# Addicted to Unhappiness

Also by Martha Heineman Pieper, Ph.D.
and William J. Pieper, M.D.

*Smart Love*

# Addicted to Unhappiness

Freeing Yourself from
Behavior that Undermines Work,
Relationships, and the Life You Want

**Martha Heineman Pieper, Ph.D.
and William J. Pieper, M.D.**

**McGraw-Hill**

New York  Chicago  San Francisco  Lisbon  London  Madrid
Mexico City  Milan  New Delhi  San Juan  Seoul
Singapore  Sydney  Toronto

The *McGraw·Hill* Companies

Library of Congress Cataloging-in-Publication Data
Pieper, Martha Heineman, 1941-
  Addicted to unhappiness : free yourself from moods and behaviors that
undermine relationships, work, and the life you want / Martha Heineman
Pieper and William J. Pieper.
      p. cm.
Includes bibliographical referensces and index.
  ISBN 0-07-138549-5 (alk. paper)
  1. Happiness.   2. Self-defeating behavior.   I. Pieper, William Joseph,
1929-II. Title
  BF575.H27 P54 2002
  158.1—dc21                                                    2002010570

1 2 3 4 5 6 7 8 9 0   AGM/AGM   0 9 8 7 6 5 4 3 2

ISBN 0-07-138549-5

The purpose of this book is to educate. It is sold with the understanding that the author and publisher
shall have neither liability nor responsibility for any injury caused or alleged to be caused directly or
indirectly by the information found in this book. While every effort has been made to ensure the book's
accuracy, its contents should not be construed as medical advice. Each person's health needs are unique.
To obtain recommendations appropriate to your particular situation, please consult a qualified health care
professional

*This book is dedicated to all our clients (past and present) — it has been our privilege to work with you.*

# Contents

# Acknowledgments

This book has been immensely improved by numerous devoted readers who, of course, bear no responsibility for any remaining imperfections. We would especially like to thank Dan Rosenberg, to whose comprehensive, creative, thoughtful comments we have happily become addicted; Fay Sawyier, our beloved and insightful first reader; and Jessica Heineman-Pieper, for her rigorous standards and sensitive reading. We are also grateful for the comments of Josef Blass, Pastora San Juan Cafferty, Jeffie Pike Durham, Natalie and Ben Heineman, Tamara Scheinfeld, Elizabeth Hersh, Jotham Stein, Victoria Heineman Stein, and the other readers who generously took the time and trouble to help us.

We are fortunate to have had the opportunity to work with Susan Clarey and Nancy Hancock, who made the editing process as enjoyable as it was productive.

# Addicted to Unhappiness

# Introduction

Most likely you are reading this book because in some way your life is not turning out exactly as you wished or hoped. While some portion of your dissatisfaction may stem from events, such as illness or social and economic upheavals, which are beyond your control, you will discover in these pages that the power to improve the most meaningful aspects of your life always remains in your own hands. Specifically, you will find that an acquired but unrecognized need to cause yourself unhappiness is undermining crucial aspects of your emotional and physical health, relationships, or work life. You will also discover that it is never too late to learn how to conquer this addiction to unhappiness and make your life significantly happier, richer, and more fulfilling.

Perhaps you are already aware that you have played some part in keeping yourself from living the life you want. You are still carrying those extra pounds you can't lose, you find yourself fighting with those you care about, you can't rebound emotionally from upsetting events, or you aren't making the most of your talents. Or maybe you are in the dark as to why you often feel restless, anxious, angry, or down, why your love life is unexciting, or why your work life is dissatisfying.

This may not be your first effort to improve your life. You may have turned to other authors or made repeated resolutions that seemed promising but petered out without bringing lasting improvements. Like so many who struggle to better their lives, you may doubt that you have the willpower to bring about significant change. Yet giving up the hope of making your life different is not an acceptable option.

When the good intentions that lead people to diet, exercise, work harder, set aside more time for their family, or get their finances in order evaporate, and leave them more or less where they started, it is not because these people are weak-willed or don't care enough about themselves. The explanation for their failure is that these people are victims of an internal struggle that is largely invisible to them, even while it is dramatically affecting them.

We call the internal forces that prevent people from living the life they want, or even from keeping a resolution that is important to them, *the addiction to unhappiness.* Even while people are consciously seeking happiness, they may unknowingly require some degree of discomfort to maintain a sense of inner balance. The unrecognized need to sabotage one's good intentions can explain diverse yet common difficulties, including overspending, fear of new situations, romantic choices that break hearts, and career mishaps.

You may well have had inklings of a need for unhappiness. You may have noticed that at times you prevent yourself from attaining goals you know you want (you get involved with the wrong person; you choose a career that makes you frustrated and unhappy). Or, when you reach your chosen goal you inexplicably sabotage it (you find the perfect person but then fight with him and drive him away; you choose the right job but are unable to make yourself meet deadlines; you lose those pounds and gain them back).

You may have felt puzzled when you achieved a goal you strove for only to find that your success didn't bring the happiness you were expecting. Perhaps the goal no longer seemed so meaningful, or your satisfaction was diminished because you found yourself dwelling on other desires that remained unfulfilled. Or maybe you suffered a severe personal loss, such as the death or illness of a loved one, and you find yourself unable to recover emotionally even though much time has passed. Perhaps you are a person who has good health, a successful career, and supportive relationships, but you nonetheless feel anxious, vaguely depressed, or lacking energy.

We are not implying that you consistently feel unhappy or frustrated. You want to enjoy your life, and no doubt you usually do feel satisfied and happy. But if you have an addiction to unhappiness then, at least occasionally, you need to cause yourself some type of discomfort in order to maintain your inner equilibrium. Whether the need for unhappiness causes you serious problems or only manifests itself in subtle ways, whether it affects you most of the time or only once in a while, nonetheless it is probably the reason you are not getting the pleasure out of life you were born to know.

*Addicted to Unhappiness* is unique in that it is both optimistic and realistic. It focuses equally on effective strategies for positive change and on combating the forces that oppose self-improvement. Unlike others who show you a path, expect you to follow it all the way to the end, and offer no help when you trip and fall, we know that the addiction to unhappiness can make change hard and backsliding inevitable. We will remain by your side for the entire journey, including the times when you waver and lose momentum and direction. In fact, one of our main goals is to show you why progress has been so difficult to sustain and how to transform reversals into opportunities for growth. Armed with that understanding, you will find that it is within your power to change your life for the better and forever.

You may be a reader who is not struggling with any particular issue in your life but who is interested in psychology and would like a better understanding of yourself and others. We have written this book for you as well, and hope that you will find it helpful and informative.

## The Genesis of *Addicted to Unhappiness*

Everyone is born with the potential to live happy, fulfilled lives, but most people find it difficult to attain that potential. Many years ago now, we set out to discover why people aren't living the life they want to have and what could be done to help them. Others had studied the discontent that is the lot of many adults and mistakenly concluded that at birth babies already possess the traits, such as selfishness, aggression toward others, and the inability to regulate appetites, that can make the adult world so unpleasant. This misperception of the newborn has done incalculable harm. For example, it led experts to advise parents to stamp out unwanted traits at an early age by making children behave like miniature adults. But demanding too much of children can teach them to expect too much of themselves and others and can make their lives as adults difficult and unsatisfying.

Our clinical practice and clinical research, combined with our experience as parents of five, taught us that in reality every baby enters the world an optimist—wanting only to love and be loved. But the question remained: what happens to babies to cause them to grow into adults who have so much difficulty sustaining good feelings about themselves, entering into mutually satisfying relationships, working effectively, and, in general, enjoying their lives? The answer emerged when we discovered the unique way in which babies and young children see the world, specifically, the way in which they evaluate the quality of the nurture they receive.

We found that all babies are born believing that their parents are perfect caregivers who want only the best for them. Every baby also wants and needs to be just like those who love and care for her. So when important adults are regularly unavailable or follow the wrong parenting advice and punish or expect too much of their children, children have no choice but to equate, unknowingly but nonetheless firmly, the unhappiness they feel with loving and being loved. Subsequently, without realizing it they periodically try to make themselves happy by re-creating this unhappiness for themselves. This confusion of unhappiness with happiness persists into adulthood and is responsible for the addiction to unhappiness that can undermine the conscious intention to seek only happiness and fulfillment.

*The reason positive change is possible is that you never lose your inborn thirst for genuine pleasure.* Genuine pleasure is to be found both in the well-founded inner certainty that you are loving and loveable, and also in the actualization of constructive, appropriate life choices.

Genuine pleasure always enhances your life—it is never harmful to you or to others.

The inborn desire for genuine pleasure always opposes the addiction to unhappiness. We know from experience that if you have an addiction to unhappiness, the information you will find in these pages will make clear how it is affecting you. Your newfound awareness that your inner well-being rests on opposing forms of happiness, one vastly inferior to the other, will empower you to choose real happiness over the false happiness that is really unhappiness in disguise.

We tested our discoveries in many settings: our own psychotherapeutic work with children, adolescents, and adults; as consultants and supervisors to mental health professionals working with a variety of clients; and in a successful state-funded project designed to demonstrate that our approach would succeed even with adolescents who had been deemed and labeled "untreatable." We consistently found our therapeutic principles to be equally effective across a range of socioeconomic, racial, ethnic, and cultural backgrounds, and with problems as diverse as depression, relationship difficulties, weight-loss struggles, and workplace issues. Most important, we know from experience that once the addiction to unhappiness is illuminated and confronted directly and persistently its influence ebbs, leaving individuals free to reclaim their birthright of undiluted happiness and fulfillment.

Our discoveries and the evidence that supports them were set down at length in *Intrapsychic Humanism: An Introduction to a Comprehensive Psychology and Philosophy of Mind*, which was written expressly for professionals and academics. As interest in *Intrapsychic Humanism* spread through the professional and academic communities, we were repeatedly asked to write a book that would apply our insights about children and childhood to helping parents. In *Smart Love: The Compassionate Alternative to Discipline That Will Make You a Better Parent and Your Child a Better Person,* we show parents that conventional parenting advice actually harms children by causing them to develop needs to make themselves and others unhappy. *Smart*

*Love* emphasizes that the potential for stable inner happiness is the birthright of every baby and offers parents practical guidelines for giving their children the special kind of love they need to grow into satisfied, fulfilled, caring adults.

We were inspired to write *Addicted to Unhappiness* by the many letters we received from adults who had read our parenting book and wanted help in applying its principles to improve their own lives. Just as *Smart Love* teaches parents how to break the negative cycle with their children and help their children regain their emotional health, this book will show you how to stop sabotaging your good intentions and, thereby, make consistently rewarding choices in your work and love life, care for your body, and regulate your moods.

The fundamental premise of *Addicted to Unhappiness* is that, in the absence of major social upheavals or oppression, the inability of most people to live the life they want results from an addiction to unhappiness. This new understanding leads to effective strategies for recognizing and vanquishing the learned need to undermine one's constructive efforts. At the same time, we encourage you to respond with compassion rather than irritation, anger, or shame to the possibility that you suffer from an addiction to unhappiness. After all, an addiction to unhappiness is not the result of weakness of will, inborn temperament, or character flaws. Paradoxically, it arises from a positive, inborn wish for relationship pleasure and inner happiness. This constructive desire can be unintentionally distorted in early childhood into the unrecognized need to feel "happy" by re-creating the familiar sort of unhappiness that comes from being punished, disapproved of, neglected, or expected too much of.

Equally important, *Addicted to Unhappiness* offers you a plan for life in that its message will not decay or lose its power over time. Its principles and guidelines will permanently protect you from the powerful pull toward self-sabotage. *Addicted to Unhappiness* puts the kind of happiness that is the birthright of every baby within your reach. This happiness consists of an inner well-being that is not vulnerable to life's ups and downs and that leads to a life filled with positive, satisfying choices.

## Organization of the Book

*Addicted to Unhappiness* is divided into two sections. The first, "Causes and Consequences of the Addiction to Unhappiness," describes the origins in early childhood of the unrecognized need to create unhappiness for oneself and details the ways in which this need can interfere in people's lives. For example, the addiction to unhappiness can cause unpleasant moods, unsatisfying relationships, and the inability to follow through on heartfelt resolutions.

The second section, "Choosing Happiness," shows you step-by-step how to use your newfound awareness of the addiction to unhappiness to improve your moods and health, to increase your satisfaction at work, and to find and enjoy close relationships. Most important, when you learn that reversals are actually part of the healing process, you will no longer need to feel ashamed or defeated by moments of backsliding. We will provide you with effective strategies for getting through and beyond the lapses that have been so destructive to your previous efforts.

Our insights and suggestions are everywhere illustrated with real-life examples drawn from our clinical experience. Naturally, we have changed the names and identifying information of our clients. Also, when we say that someone "saw us," we mean that the person saw one of us, not that the person met with both of us. We do not specify which of us the person consulted to provide more privacy for our clients.

The phases in overcoming the addiction to unhappiness are Getting Started (Even When You Don't Feel Like It), Coping with Episodes of Backsliding, Keeping Your Resolve When It Starts to Evaporate, and Thinking of Yourself as a Recovering Addict to Unhappiness. You will find concrete strategies for navigating these phases successfully in whatever area of your life you want to improve. We offer strategies for freeing yourself from painful moods, making an ongoing commitment to take good care of your body, building relationships based on closeness rather than conflict, and finding happiness at work. Our program is a blueprint you can follow for the rest of your life. Because it incorporates the reality that plateaus and backsliding are a part of all successful change, its message will not decay or lose its potency over time.

# Section I

# Causes and Consequences of the Addiction to Unhappiness

There are any number of ways in which people can prevent themselves from being the person they want to be and from having the life they want to have. If you recognize yourself in one or more of the following predicaments, then to some degree you are addicted to unhappiness. We emphasize that the addiction to unhappiness affects different people in different ways. Its consequences can be relatively minor or they can be grave and disabling; they may appear in only one aspect of someone's life or they can permeate a person's day-to-day experience.

*Predicament:* I am unable to sustain a resolution, whether the resolve is to lose weight, keep my temper, or get my work done on time. An advertising executive told us, "Even though my doctor told me to lose weight because I have high blood pressure, I cannot seem to do it. I lose a few pounds and then gain them right back."

*Predicament:* I feel devastated and find it hard to bounce back when things go badly. A woman confided, "When my boss made a critical remark on a Friday about a report I had prepared, I could not get his words out of my mind. I felt crushed and ashamed all weekend and could barely manage to relate to the other members of my family. I knew I was overreacting, but I could not shake the misery I was feeling."

*Predicament:* I snatch defeat from the jaws of victory—just as the success I have worked tirelessly to achieve is within my grasp, I do something to let it slip. A college student told us that she had slaved over an assignment only to find that she had left it in her dorm the day it was due, with the result that her "A" paper was marked down a grade.

*Predicament:* I achieve success and then lose it. A professional tennis player came to us because he could play his best only until he achieved a considerable lead over his opponent. Then he would make unforced errors and either lose the match altogether or have to expend tremendous effort to work his way out of the hole he had dug for himself.

*Predicament:* I achieve a goal I have worked hard for, but I find I can't seem to enjoy it. Either it doesn't seem as important as I thought it was when I was pursuing it or I focus on some other desire that remains unfulfilled. A lawyer we know enjoyed working the 70-hour weeks necessary for him to become a partner in his law firm. Immediately after he became a partner, however, he felt bored and restless practicing law and began to think seriously about changing careers.

*Predicament:* I have trouble forming close, meaningful relationships. A woman we know was drawn to relationships with people who wanted less involvement than she did, with the result that she often felt hurt and rejected. A man we were seeing habitually chose partners and friends who were abusive, substance addicted, or otherwise certain to make him miserable.

*Predicament:* When I find someone who cares about me as much as I care about her, I create conflict and ruin the relationship. A contractor spent many years searching for the woman of his dreams. When he finally found her, he enjoyed a brief period of genuine closeness. Then he found himself picking fights with her over insignificant issues, such as what movie to see or her taste in clothes. He asked us to help him before he ruined the relationship altogether.

*Predicament:* I can never seem to get my work done well or on time: I frequently procrastinate; I find it hard to concentrate; I have difficulty being thorough; I have trouble meeting deadlines.

*Predicament:* I work too hard and can't allow myself to have or to enjoy recreational time or time with my family. An accountant came to us for help because he was getting close to retirement and realized that he was terrified at the thought of the unstructured time stretching before him. He had hardly taken a day off from his job because he felt restless and anxious when he wasn't at work.

*Predicament:* The activities I most enjoy are risky. I worry that I may harm myself, but I can't bring myself to give up the pleasure I get from these activities. An avid motorcycle racer came to us because he had had a number of close calls, his wife was about to give birth to their first child, and he did not want to miss seeing his child grow up. Yet he was torn because he was convinced that he couldn't get the thrill he felt when he raced in any other way.

*Predicament:* I am frequently plagued by unpleasant emotions. A businesswoman came to see us because for no apparent reason she often felt painfully anxious and depressed.

*Predicament:* I don't feel passionately about anything and wonder, "What's it all about?" A woman jumped from job to job, relationship to relationship, activity to activity, searching for a feeling of fulfillment and purpose. When she continued to feel dissatisfied, she sought our help.

*Predicament:* I have experienced significant personal losses from which I can't seem to recover. One woman whose husband had been killed in a car accident three years previously came to see us because her daily bouts of tearfulness and depression were not abating.

*Predicament:* I cannot regulate my appetites (for food, drink, gambling, sex, etc.). A photographer was referred to us by his wife because he spent every evening drinking one beer after another. He told us that it was the only way he had of unwinding after a day of hard work.

If you have struggled with these or similar difficulties, you have experienced firsthand the workings of the addiction to unhappiness. In the pages that follow we first show you in more detail why and how the addiction to unhappiness can sabotage your good intentions, your positive choices, and your inner equilibrium, and then we describe the strategies that will make it possible for you to overcome this addiction and to choose happiness once and for all.

## Understanding Your Childhood Years Is the Key to Making Changes in Your Life Today

We are going to take you on a brief journey that will touch on selected aspects of your childhood. We recognize that as an adult with pressing problems and the desire to make your life better in the here and now, you may feel perplexed and maybe even a little frustrated at the prospect of looking back in time. The reason we dwell at some length on your early experiences is that they live on to interfere in unseen ways with your ability to create the life you want. Before you can make lasting and meaningful improvements in your life, you have to recognize and understand the roadblocks that are keeping you from the happiness you were born to know.

In your way are negative assumptions about yourself and others that you most likely learned before you could talk and certainly before you had a mind that was even close to the mind you now possess. These assumptions may be invisible to you, but they are as real as stones and they exert tremendous influence. The good news is that a careful reading of these pages can uncover and defuse these negative assumptions, empowering you to lead the life you want.

Thinkers as diverse as Socrates, St. Augustine, Shakespeare, and Freud have recognized that our childhood experiences have a profound effect on our adult lives. However, because our most influential experiences occurred before we could organize and remember them in the language we speak today, the exact nature of the young child's mind has remained a mystery. For the first time a window into the young child's experience is made possible by our discovery that all babies enter the world as optimists who love their parents and believe their parents are perfect and perfectly devoted to them. The momentous consequence of this new understanding of babies' immature outlook is that it is impossible for them to evaluate the quality of the parenting they receive. Our most important discovery is this: *We are all born to love whatever care we get and to want more of it.*

It is not our intention to blame parents or other adults who were important to you. Your caregivers did the best they could and, certainly, they wanted nothing but the best for you. We dwell on your childhood experiences because the only way permanently to change your life for the better is to understand why and how the effects of these experiences are influencing you today.

# Chapter 1

# Confusing Unhappiness
with Happiness

By far the most common view of the newborn comes down to us over many centuries of Western culture, namely, that babies are born sinful or as otherwise antisocial beings who are inclined to manipulate their parents. We have found this view to be fundamentally misleading. Equally misleading are three other popular views: children are born as blank slates that passively soak up experience; children are born in a state of innocence that is soon corrupted or shattered by the sinfulness of the world; and children are born with personalities that are already "hardwired."

The truth is that all newborns enter the world optimists about human relationships, adoring their parents, and certain that they are so loveable that they are causing their parents to love caring for them. *Children also believe that everything they experience, both good and bad, is an expression of the love they need because it is what their parents want for them.* Because they love their parents so completely, they want nothing more than to grow up to be just like them and to treat themselves just as they are treated.

In other words, you did not come into the world antisocial, manipulative, tending to be spoiled and dependent, blank, or unable to distinguish your parents from yourself. Nor did your genes cause the character traits that make your life difficult.

## Your Birthright of Happiness

Every child is born with a starter supply of inner happiness—feeling loveable, loving, and loved. All children, including blind and deaf children, give evidence of this inborn happiness when within a few weeks of birth they begin to smile somewhat indiscriminately whenever they feel they have caused their parents' loving attention and, thereby, made themselves particularly happy. As the first three months pass, babies increasingly identify special faces as the source of their greatest pleasure. The ecstatic grin that they save especially for their parents indicates that they are delighted both with their parents and with themselves for causing their parents to love them.

Over time the inborn well-being of children who receive informed parenting becomes rock solid and cannot be shaken regardless of the ups and downs that occur in a person's life. Certainly anyone who experiences a significant loss or disappointment will feel sad, but those whose inner happiness is stable will not have developed a need to turn on themselves or others for comfort when things do not go well. Because those persons will have no need to cause themselves *any* kind of unnecessary unhappiness, they will also make good choices and will be able consistently to follow through on these choices.

In other words, your birthright and the birthright of every child is a kind of nurture that makes permanent your inborn conviction of being loveable and loved. The result is a lifelong ability to take good care of yourself and your body, the knack of choosing and keeping loyal friends and partners, the capacity to work to your potential and enjoy it, the resilience to recover from setbacks and bad luck, and the ability to give your own children the gift of inner happiness. This is not a utopian view. Everyone has the potential for this kind of adulthood. And, as we are going to show you, *the good news is that it is never too late.* Even if you missed this type of happiness the first time around, we will show you how to create it for yourself from this moment forward.

# The Root of the Confusion

If you are trying to improve the quality of your life, the first step in taking charge of your destiny is to understand why you aren't entirely in charge of yourself now. *The startling but simple truth is that, like most people without meaning to, on occasion you probably make your life difficult or unhappy because your love for your parents caused you to confuse happiness and unhappiness.* In order to know how this can be so, you need to understand the special way in which you saw the world as an infant.

## You Were a Born Imitator

At birth your eyes focused at just the right distance to light on your parents' faces as they smiled at you and talked to you. You were born knowing your mother's voice and finding it soothing. Also, you entered the world with an amazing talent. Having never seen your own face, you could copy your parents' facial gestures. For example, if your father opened his mouth or stuck out his tongue, you could figure out how to make your face look just like his face by opening your mouth or sticking out your tongue.

Your desire to be just like your parents didn't stop with trying to look like them. Because you adored your parents and thought they were perfect, you wanted to *be* exactly like them. One way to be like them was to try to make yourself feel exactly the way they made you feel. So when you cried because you were hungry or tired and your parents fed you or helped you to get to sleep, you developed powerful needs to treat yourself and others with the same kind of love and devotion.

When parents are able to meet their children's emotional needs sufficiently to preserve and strengthen their children's inborn optimism, children learn to make themselves happy by re-creating the compassion and kindness they receive. Their inner happiness—the deep conviction of being loveable, loved, and loving—is continually reaffirmed by their parents' responsiveness until it becomes unshakable. An unshakable and stable inner happiness, the birthright of each of us, protects its possessors from ever knowingly or unknowingly making their lives or the lives of others difficult or unhappy.

But what if, with all the good intentions in the world, your parents could not reliably respond to your emotional needs because they didn't understand them or for some reason were prevented from satisfying them? The most common failures to meet children's emotional needs arise from leaving unhappy infants and children to cry, expecting too much of children, and disciplining children.

### The Connection Between Being Left to Cry and Needing Unhappiness to Feel Completely Happy

Let's say that your parents were following popular but harmful advice to let you cry yourself to sleep. (We could have chosen any other example of parents letting babies and young children cry in the belief that misery is harmless, provides relief, or builds character.) Like all babies, you often got overtired or overstimulated, and you needed some soothing to help you relax and sleep. Your parents may have been told that you were crying to manipulate them, to exercise your lungs, to relieve tension, or as a way of getting to sleep, but none of this is true. *You cried as a baby for the same reason you cry as an adult—you were unhappy.*

If you cried when you were put in your crib to sleep and your parents left you to cry by yourself, their absence made you feel even more miserable because your certainty of being loveable and loved crumbled. Soon you were crying for two very different reasons. You were still suffering from the discomfort of being overtired, of having indigestion, or of experiencing some other kind of distress. Worse yet, you were feeling miserable because the people you loved and adored above all else in life weren't coming to your rescue. Eventually, when your cries for help went unanswered for what seemed an eternity, you gave up trying to attract your parents' attention and you fell asleep. When you slept, your parents probably concluded that the experts' advice to let you cry yourself to sleep was well-founded. What they didn't know was that by focusing on getting you to behave in a certain way (to go to sleep quickly), rather than on showing you that you could always count for help on their loving presence, they were setting you on a path that could end with your need to make your life unnecessarily difficult and unpleasant.

A subtle transformation occurs in sleepless, hungry, colicky, or overtired infants who are left to cry "for their own good." Infants who are left to cry assume that their unhappiness is desirable because it is what their parents want them to feel. The same process occurs in older children whose parents ignore them when they are having tantrums or when they are unhappy at other times and in other ways that their parents and other important adults don't understand or don't approve of. When their unhappiness goes uncomforted children remain convinced that their parents are giving them ideal love, with the result that they confuse the unhappiness they experience with happiness. This misidentification preserves the inner conviction of being worthwhile that is necessary to maintain life. But the consequence is that without knowing it, these children grow up to feel a sense of well-being when they re-create experiences of unhappiness for themselves. In other words, they develop an addiction to unhappiness that coexists and competes with their inborn need to experience genuine happiness.

So, if in your earliest years your tears were not responded to, rather than realizing as an objective observer would that you were miserable, you believed that uncomforted unhappiness was the ideal state that the parents you worshipped wanted you to experience. Concluding that these unhappy feelings represented true happiness, you naturally developed a strong desire or need to re-create them. As you grew older, you may unknowingly have begun to feel that since these unhappy feelings were what your parents wanted you to feel, you were betraying or disappointing your parents if you felt too happy.

Thus, while still very young, children whose emotional needs are not met develop two very different sources of inner well-being: (1) the inborn pleasure of feeling loveable and loved and (2) feelings of unhappiness that they unknowingly misidentify as happiness and that they seek out in order to reexperience the feelings they believe their parents want them to feel.

If your tears regularly went uncomforted, then from a very early age, before you could reason, have any realistic idea what was in someone else's mind, or have a standard of comparison to measure the caregiving you got against the caregiving you needed, you had an unrecognized but very real inner conflict about the best way to feel happy. You needed to make yourself truly happy, but you also needed to provide yourself with false happiness, which is really unhappiness in disguise.

We emphasize that it really doesn't matter whether you were left to cry because you couldn't sleep, because you were hungry and it wasn't "time" for the next feeding, because your stomach hurt from colic and your parents were told you would feel better if you relieved your tension by crying, or because you couldn't have your older brother's toy. The result was the same. Some of the time, deep inside, in a completely unrecognized manner, without meaning to or wanting to, you soothed yourself with unhappiness masquerading as happiness. Understanding this is the first step in recovering from the addiction to unhappiness and getting on with your life.

### The Connection Between What Was Expected of You and Your Need to Demand Too Much of Yourself and Others

Like every child, you needed your parents to know what your essential needs were at every age and to respond to those needs in a reliable manner. Yet your parents may have had trouble meeting your needs because, like other parents, they were told to expect a level of maturity from you that does not fit with the way a child's mind really develops. If you are one of the many people who periodically suffer from feelings of insecurity and inadequacy, it is likely that too much was expected of you as a child, with the result that you grew up feeling that you were frequently disappointing your parents and other important adults.

Your parents (and, later, your teachers) may have believed that if you were to turn out well, they had to civilize you early and often. Most parents are taught that children will grow into adults who enact the same social behaviors they exhibit as children. They think that if an eight-year-old gets upset when he loses a game, he must be taught to be a good sport or else he will grow up to be a poor loser. Similarly, parents are misadvised that traits that are desirable in adults, such as generosity and responsibility, have to be taught early or they will never be learned. Most children are expected, early on, to be truthful, to be a caring sibling, a good loser, a good eater, and a consistent chore-doer.

What your parents and teachers didn't know was how different your mind was from theirs. An adult who experiences anger or disapproval from another can evaluate the reasonableness of the other's behavior. But when children are punished or faced with disapproval for not living up to expectations that are too high, even though they may feel angry, underneath they always believe that their parents are perfect and that whatever their parents do is right. As a result they conclude that whatever unhappiness they feel is what their parents intend, and that they will be happiest if they become just like their parents and treat themselves and others exactly as their parents treated them.

Your parents and teachers were misguidedly trying to make you act like an adult. However, you were unable to behave like an adult because, like all children, your everyday happiness depended to a large extent on getting what you wanted when you wanted it. This is why as a two-year-old it was practically impossible to share with other children, why as a three-year-old you cried when it was raining and you couldn't go to the park, why as a six-year-old you didn't always tell the truth about how many pieces of candy you had eaten, and why you felt so upset as an eight-year-old when you lost a game.

If your parents had known that, like all children, your self-esteem was dependent to some extent on having things go your way, and that this vulnerability to disappointments would be outgrown naturally, then they would have felt free to comfort you in a relaxed manner when you became upset. When you melted down or bent the truth, they would not have worried that too much understanding or sympathy would cause you to grow into an adult who was selfish, untruthful, or a bad sport. You would have learned gradually that even though things did not always turn out as you wished, you could always count on the pleasure of being understood and comforted by those you loved. Sympathetic responses would have made getting your way seem less important and would have hastened your development into a caring, sharing adult. You would also have emulated your parents and learned to offer sympathy and understanding to yourself and others when disappointments occurred.

But if your parents or teachers misunderstood what it is to have the mind of a child and expected you to show a maturity of which you weren't capable, you agreed with them that you *should* be able to act as they wished and you felt inadequate. You had no way to determine what was a reasonable expectation, so you may still expect more of yourself than is fair, and you may often find it difficult to feel that your efforts are good enough. Even though it is painful and uncomfortable, deep down expecting too much of yourself also brings you the pleasure of false happiness (unhappiness you long ago confused with happiness). When you treat yourself the way you were treated by your parents and important others, you feel like them and, therefore, loved by them and loveable.

## Jennifer

Jennifer worked for a company that conducted public opinion polls for politicians. She and another woman, Carol, selected the population samples, went into the field together, did interviews, entered the data they gathered into the computer, and then analyzed it. Each of these steps was fraught with possibilities for error. Jennifer was junior to Carol and looked to her for help, especially around the sophisticated problems that arose collecting and analyzing the data. Carol always seemed willing to assist her. Then Jennifer learned from Jill, a secretary in the office, that Carol complained to Jennifer's coworkers and her boss that Jennifer was "needy" and a "slow learner." Jennifer felt devastated by these remarks and rebuked herself severely for her inability to get up-to-speed quickly. The less competent Jennifer felt, the more she turned to Carol for advice, and the more she heard from Jill that Carol was complaining about her to her office mates. Jennifer began to feel that the job she had worked so hard to get and had thought she would enjoy was beyond her. Jennifer was on the verge of resigning when she consulted us.

It was immediately clear to us that Jennifer suffered from a persistent sense of inadequacy that clouded the reality that she was extremely bright and a good learner. She had done very well in school even though she had never felt as intelligent as her classmates. She said, "I was always convinced that I was going to fail all of my courses, and I was always amazed when I got good grades."

Jennifer had grown up in a home with clear expectations: She was to be polite; she was to be an "A" student; she was to help out regularly around the house; she was to baby-sit for her younger siblings when her parents went out; and she was not to complain. Jennifer adored her parents, was gratified by their faith in her, and tried her best to live up to the standards they set. When inevitably she fell short, it never occurred to her that the problem was that the expectations were too high for any child. She felt that she was woefully lacking and felt shame at disappointing her parents. No wonder, then, that Jennifer wholeheartedly accepted Carol's criticisms at face value.

As we continued our work together, Jennifer often felt that she was letting us down by not progressing more quickly. When she learned that she had adopted the unrealistic expectations toward herself that had shaped her childhood, she thought that this understanding would cause her feelings of inadequacy immediately to disappear. When they persisted, she felt that she was unsuited to the work we were doing and that we were disappointed in her because she was not moving along faster. Jennifer was surprised when we explained that her feelings of inadequacy would not disappear overnight. Painful as these feelings were, they were also a source of false happiness. Jennifer was trying to feel the way she had believed her parents meant for her to feel. When she felt inadequate, deep down she also felt cared for and worthwhile. Jennifer told us, "For the first time I can see what a difference it would have made if I had grown up with expectations I could actually meet."

Through her work with us, Jennifer began to understand that Carol was not an accurate judge of Jennifer's performance, but was a person whose own addiction to unhappiness drove her to depreciate those with a reasonable and indeed a healthy motive to get help from her. Jennifer saw that anyone starting a job as complex as the one she had would need guidance, and that her questions had been neither stupid nor unnecessary. She avoided Carol and instead sought advice from another woman in the office who was comfortable in the role of mentor. Shortly thereafter, Jennifer asked for and was given a different partner. Her work and her confidence level improved, and for the first time she thoroughly enjoyed her job.

If you make a concerted and largely successful effort to attain a goal and find that instead of feeling proud of your accomplishment you focus on the one or two aspects of your effort that could have been better, you are importing into your adult life the perfectionistic standard you embraced as a child. When parents pressure their children to excel or to behave with the social graces of adults, children understandably but mistakenly conclude that their parents want perfection. As a result, children grow up feeling good about themselves when they impose even more exacting requirements on themselves than the erroneous standards their parents were using. If you have overly strict expectations for yourself and others, identifying the roots of these expectations is the first step toward freeing yourself from this type of addiction to unhappiness and living a life in which you consistently feel competent rather than inadequate.

Children can also feel burdened by parents' expectations even when parents do not openly demand too much of them. When parents are severely depressed, substance addicted, or otherwise dysfunctional, children may interpret occasions when their parents are unable to respond with love and caring as representing parents' wishes that their children help them, take over some of their responsibilities, or not demand caregiving for themselves.

Often the only way these children can regularly get the positive attention they need from parents who are finding it difficult to function is to become a source of emotional strength or practical help—in other words, to adopt behaviors that are way beyond their years. For example, children may get a positive response from a dysfunctional parent by assuming responsibility for chores such as cooking, cleaning, or helping with younger siblings. Children may also learn that they can improve a parent's mood and thereby get some emotional nourishment for themselves by entertaining their parents or tending to them. Most significant, these children typically learn that they feel more accepted by dysfunctional parents (and therefore happier) if they forgo asking these parents to meet any of their own needs.

As adults these children may seek relationship pleasure by involving themselves with friends or partners who need saving. They tend to feel most comfortable in one-sided relationships in which they completely devote themselves to helping their friends or partners become more functional. "Rescuers" are accustomed to providing a hundred percent of the effort that goes into a relationship, and they may overlook the reality that they are not getting much, if any, attention back from their partner. Sometimes rescuers realize that the relationship is one-sided, but they believe that they will be able to transform the other person into a friend or partner who will be more capable of giving to them. Other rescuers assume that it is normal to be in a relationship in which all the giving goes in one direction.

### Judy

*Judy, an administrative assistant in her early thirties, was living with and engaged to Tom, a man who regularly gambled away everything he made. Judy felt it was her job to help Tom overcome his gambling problem. She tried to convince him to give her part of his paycheck to hold, but Tom became indignant. When he spent all his money and begged for hers, she often gave in and let him have as much of her earnings as she could spare. Judy had to put in many extra hours at her own job to earn the money to cover Tom's half of the rent, and to save for their wedding and for a down payment on the house they wanted to buy.*

*While Judy felt strongly that loving Tom meant accepting him as he was, she could see that marrying him would mean committing herself to a life in which she would be the breadwinner. Moreover, she was concerned that once they were married she would be legally responsible for paying back whatever money Tom could borrow for gambling. These debts might well ruin her good credit and sink her financially.*

*Her friends were aware of Tom's gambling problem and urged her to get professional advice before she married him. When she came to see us, Judy immediately shared the fact that she had grown up with an alcoholic father. She said, "It seems as though I spent my entire childhood tiptoeing around my father when he was drinking. The only way I ever got a smile or a pat on the head from him was when I brought him a sandwich and his paper, or picked up empty glasses and plates." Judy's mother regularly made excuses for her husband, telling the children to leave him alone, saying "He needs to relax after a hard day at work."*

In our first sessions together, Judy was very defensive about her relationship with Tom. She dwelt on the fun they had together and how well he treated her.

Then Judy inquired, "Why aren't you as negative about Tom as my friends are?" We replied that what she decided about Tom was entirely up to her, we were just there to help her discover what she really wanted. Judy admitted to being confused. She said, "I feel selfish and disloyal whenever I think about leaving Tom. I worry about what will become of him. And if I break up with him, I know I would miss him terribly. But I also don't like the thought of supporting him and assuming his debts." Judy had suppressed her negative feelings by convincing herself that Tom would change, but as two years had passed and he had only gotten deeper in debt, she had become less hopeful.

As we got to know Judy, we realized that she had difficulty sharing her feelings. She would tell us about an incident that was upsetting to her, but she didn't express strong emotions of any kind, and she quickly changed the subject. When we remarked on this pattern, she said that she didn't want to burden us. She stated that since we were hearing other people's unhappy feelings all day long, she hesitated to bother us with her own troubles.

We helped Judy to see that, without realizing it, she was trying to make herself feel better by forgoing her needs for our help and trying to take care of us, just as she had done with her father. We made clear that we were ready and willing to give her the assistance she needed. At first Judy had trouble believing that she could get help for herself without having to take care of us. Little by little, she became able to share her thoughts and feelings without worrying about the effect they would have on us. As she experienced the pleasure of having her own needs met, she felt increasingly less satisfied with her relationship with Tom. Finally, she concluded that she did not want to spend the rest of her life taking care of him without getting much in return. She decided that she wanted to continue working with us in order to gain the ability to participate in a truly mutual relationship.

Rescue-based relationships frequently continue for many years. Because rescuers often take responsibility for the other person's problems, rescuers may respond by redoubling their efforts when the other person doesn't change. Also, because as children they confused the pain caused by sacrificing their own needs with the happiness of genuine love, rescuers tend to feel good about themselves when they remain in this kind of relationship.

If you are a person who tends to get involved in relationships based on saving the other person, in Chapter 6, Building Relationships Based on Closeness, Not Conflict, we will help you identify these relationships and give you strategies and guidelines for improving them or knowing how and when to leave them.

## The Connection Between Being Disciplined and Responding Harshly to Yourself and Others

If you were disciplined as a child, the emotional consequences you suffered may be another piece in the puzzle of why your life is not turning out as you wished. *We define discipline as attaching unpleasant consequences to the management of children's behavior.* We include in this definition of discipline not just punishments, but any responses to children that make them feel inadequate, ashamed, or naughty. Disciplinary measures include disapproval, time-outs, restriction of privileges, standing by and allowing "natural consequences" to occur, lectures, slapping, and spanking.

Until now, you may have thought that the discipline you received was deserved because it was necessary to control your behavior or build your character. But our finding is that any and all discipline harms children by creating in them needs to be disciplinarians toward themselves and others. Since all young children believe their parents are perfect and know what is good for them, by definition children who are regularly disciplined unknowingly conclude that the unhappiness that follows is desirable. Because children also have an inborn need to emulate their parents, they develop needs to re-create the "happiness" they feel when they are disciplined, which really involves making themselves unhappy in some way. As adults, they may turn on themselves or they may involve themselves with friends or partners who treat them badly or whom they treat badly.

### Loving Regulation: The Positive Alternative to Discipline and Permissiveness

When we wrote our parenting book, most parents were not aware that there was an alternative to discipline other than permissiveness. We showed parents that the intended goal of discipline, namely, being in charge of a child, can be achieved much more effectively if parents avoid imposing any sort of negative consequence. Being in charge of a child is imperative—all children need to be protected from their immaturity. They must take their medicine, ride in car seats, be stopped from sailing toy boats in the toilet, and be prevented from trashing their siblings' rooms. But children can be managed without unpleasantness.

We call this way of keeping children safe and sound without punishing or disapproving of them *loving regulation*, which we define as *managing children's behavior without adding additional unhappiness or depriving children of parental warmth and admiration*. Time-outs, restrictions, punishments, and other forms of discipline are based on the assumption that being too nice to children who are "misbehaving" will encourage and reward the bad behavior. But discipline harms children in the process of regulating them because it interferes with the most consistent and satisfying source of young children's inner well-being—their conviction that they are causing their parents' unconditional love of caring for them. For this reason, disciplining children makes them *more* miserable and *less* able to forgo their wishes. In contrast, loving regulation shows children that while they may have to give up a desired gratification, they can always rely on the pleasure available in the parent–child relationship.

Loving regulation is far superior to discipline because it preserves the warmth and closeness all children want and need to experience with their parents and other important adults. When children copy parents who use loving regulation, they develop the ability to provide themselves with a genuine happiness that is untainted by discomfort or other painful emotions.

Managing your behavior presented a potential problem to your parents the moment you began to move on your own. No longer could your parents put you down, confident that they could turn their backs and find you in the same place. Previously, the most difficult parenting problem your parents faced was what to do when you were unhappy. Now they were confronted with the dilemma, which would be with them until you entered adulthood, of what to do when your choice of actions and their wishes were in conflict.

You, of course, were thrilled to be on the move. Increasingly, you were able to reach those interesting objects on the living room table, to pull the tail that waved so alluringly at the end of the cat, and to try to cook on the real stove just like Mommy and Daddy. If your parents understood that you were filled with curiosity but possessed a mind too immature to comprehend danger to yourself or harm to others' possessions, they would have baby-proofed the house and lifted you from impending trouble with a hug and a kiss. Your curiosity, so important to your later learning, would not have been dampened. You would have found that while you couldn't always do what you wanted, your parents would lovingly help you find another activity that would make you happy. You would have learned that you could disagree with those you loved without losing their love and admiration.

### Discipline Teaches Children to Treat Themselves and Others Harshly

Not only were your parents probably told that you should behave with the manners and social virtues of an adult, but most likely they were also advised to enforce these unrealistic expectations with a series of disciplinary measures. These punishments ranged from disapproving statements, to time-outs, to standing by and letting "natural" consequences happen to you, to yelling "No!" to slapping or spanking. The irony is that the *worst* way to teach children altruism, safety rules, and respect for others is to discipline them for not exhibiting these behaviors. Since young children have minds that don't understand that vases break, stoves hurt, and cats' tails are sensitive to pain, they can't make sense of their parents' disapproval and punishments. Older children are often disciplined for behavior that is, in reality, normal and appropriate to their age, such as the occasional mistruth, getting upset when they can't have their way, leaving chores undone, leaving food on their plate, and being a poor loser.

Even though the discipline children receive feels unpleasant, because children adore their parents, it also feels deserved. As they grow older, children believe they are doing something good for themselves when, like their parents, they make themselves unhappy by disapproving of themselves and punishing themselves when they do something "wrong."

If your parents turned to discipline, their purpose was to teach you to stay safe, to be careful of property, to be polite, to be responsible, and to be kind to others. Without realizing it, what you really learned was that might makes right, that aggression is an effective way to solve relationship differences, and that it is good to feel negatively about yourself and about those who don't do what you want. These lessons could come back to haunt you later.

### Sarah
*Sarah came to see us because of the difficulty she was having managing employees in the small greeting card business she owned. She realized that personnel problems were undercutting the tremendous effort she was putting in to make the business a success. In spite of herself, when someone who worked for her made a mistake, Sarah became furious and was icy to the employee for weeks afterward. This negative and chilly atmosphere affected her workers. They turned sullen and many of them left for other jobs.*

*With our help, Sarah began to see that without realizing it she was making her employees feel the way she had felt when, as a child, she was disciplined for doing something "wrong." Although for a long time she continued to feel furious with employees who made mistakes, Sarah now understood that when she felt disappointed in an employee she turned to angry feelings for the comfort of feeling that she was doing the right thing in responding like her parents.*

*Gradually and with much difficulty, Sarah developed the ability to give up the familiar security of turning to anger when someone did something she didn't like. She learned to sit down with the person, to clear the air with a productive discussion, and to move on.*

If your parents and other important adults tried to get you to adopt the behaviors, manners, and morals of a grown-up, as so many experts advised them to do, and then responded to your inevitable shortcomings with disapproval and punishments, *there was no way for you to know that you were in effect being punished for being a child and having a child's mind.* If you were forced to share with other children before you were ready, were given a time-out or worse when you cried because you couldn't have the toy you wanted, lost privileges when you bent the truth to make reality more congenial, were shamed or sent to your room when you reacted angrily to losing a game, or were grounded when you didn't get your chores finished on time, you felt upset.

Simultaneously, at some level you agreed that your upset and angry feelings were unacceptable, that somehow you didn't measure up to your beloved parents' expectations, and that you deserved the discipline you received. Gradually, you learned that it could feel comforting to respond to your "failures" with self-criticism and to punish or disapprove of others who didn't behave as you wished.

### Tracy

*Tracy came to see us because, without wanting to, she was becoming increasingly irritable and angry with her fourth grade class. She had* laid down a series of expectations at the beginning of the year and was increasingly frustrated at her class's inability to follow these rules, which included: no talking to each other except in free periods or cooperative work, no interrupting other children, no talking without raising a hand and being called on, and no passing notes. Children who violated a rule were given a time-out. If they continued to break rules they were given extra homework, sent to the principal, or made to stay after school. When none of these measures seemed to work, Tracy escalated her response. If one child broke a rule, she made the entire class put their heads on their desks and spend 10 minutes in silence. Soon a substantial amount of class time was consumed by punishments, yet the infractions continued. When Tracy found herself losing her temper and screaming, she realized that she had lost control of the situation and she consulted us.

Initially, Tracy focused on her anger at her class. She insisted, "Every one of my students is perfectly able to follow the rules. They are violating them in order to get to me." When we suggested that the rules might be demanding more self-restraint than normal fourth graders could manage, Tracy vehemently disagreed. She recounted many incidents from her childhood in which much more was expected of her than she asked of her class. For example, from the time she was in preschool, her parents had insisted that she never "talk back," that she never interrupt, that she clean up her room and make her bed every day, and that she eat everything on her plate. When she broke one of these rules, she was given a time-out or other restriction. As she grew older, she was disciplined by being grounded or by having her allowance taken away for a period of time. She said, "I believe that my parents' disciplinary measures taught me to behave properly. I just can't understand why the same approach isn't working in my classroom."

When we explained that, without meaning to, her parents in effect had been punishing her for being a child, Tracy initially felt confused. While she had been ashamed that she couldn't live up to the standard her parents had set for her, she had accepted their expectations as reasonable and had tried her hardest to meet them. Moreover, she felt virtuous (happy) when she applied these standards to herself.

When Tracy began to understand more about how children develop, she saw that many of the childhood punishments she received were in response to her childish curiosity, enthusiasm, or immaturity rather than to willful misbehavior. For example, she was amazed to hear that it is normal for young children to bend the truth occasionally to make reality fit their wishes.

"One time, when I was seven, I remember that I lied to my parents," she told us. "My mother had left a piece of cake sitting on the kitchen counter, and I swore that I hadn't eaten it. My parents found the crumbs in my bedroom and docked my allowance for two weeks."

Tracy had felt mortified. "If my parents had only known that it is normal for children to bend the truth," she said, "I wouldn't have felt like such a criminal—and I would have grown up to be truthful anyway!"

By now, Tracy was ready to apply her newfound understanding to her teaching. She saw that without realizing it, when she expected too much of her class she felt she was caring for them and expressing her belief in their capabilities just as she had thought her parents' expectations represented their confidence in her. She took a fresh look at her rules and eliminated the ones that were stifling the children's creativity and enthusiasm. For example, when she lifted the bans on interrupting and on speaking without raising a hand, the class discussions became much livelier and more children participated in them.

Those rules she considered necessary for classroom order she now thought of as guidelines. When infractions occurred, she gave reminders rather than punishments and moved on. At times her old mind-set reasserted itself and she felt impelled to be angry or punitive, but she then felt free to apologize to the class for overreacting, and to say that she was having a bad day.

Tracy was thrilled to discover that her classroom experience was utterly transformed. Instead of feeling like a prison guard, she developed a learning partnership with her class. Now that she didn't have to try to enforce impossible standards of class decorum, she had extra time to concentrate on creative teaching methods. The students in her class blossomed, and they often silenced classmates who were disrupting an enjoyable group project. With her classroom a source of enjoyment rather than suffering, Tracy now turned the focus of her work with us to the ways in which her needs to expect too much of herself and others were interfering in her personal life.

If you were regularly disciplined as a child, you learned lessons very different from those your parents thought they were teaching you. Most likely, you agreed that you deserved to suffer for your mistakes. When your parents disciplined you, they were only trying to change your behavior. They did not intend for you to grow up overly critical of yourself and others.

## Joe

Joe was passed over for a promotion for which he had worked hard. He felt overcome by shame and could not bring himself to tell his wife about his disappointment because he assumed that she would feel as unsympathetic toward him as he felt toward himself. He developed a dull stomachache that went on for days. When two weeks passed with no relief from his stomachache or his misery, he sought help. When we first saw Joe, he was so ashamed of not getting the promotion that he could only say that he had experienced "disappointments at work."

When he developed enough trust to tell us what had happened, we helped Joe to realize that the shame he felt was not his just dessert, but was his special way of trying to comfort himself over the loss of his promotion. He was in effect parenting himself by striving to re-create the painful feelings he had experienced when he was disciplined as a child. Naturally, he was convinced that others would feel as negatively toward him as he did toward himself.

As he began to understand that he was heaping misery on himself in a misguided attempt to feel better, Joe was able to respond more *constructively. He gave a lot of thought to improving his performance at work, began quietly to look around for jobs that offered greater opportunities for advancement, and shared the bad news with his wife, who was very understanding.*

*Equally important, Joe realized that he was vulnerable to causing himself this kind of unhappiness whenever anything went wrong. When a disappointment occurred, he became increasingly able to recognize and then to insulate himself against the feeling that he deserved to suffer. Sometimes Joe would have nightmares after experiencing a particularly keen disappointment. We showed him that his nightmares were a sign of progress, because they were a much preferable outlet for his needs to make himself miserable than torturing himself during his waking hours.*

When parents follow popular advice to withhold privileges from children who behave in ways parents find unacceptable, their children often become adults who are inclined to turn to self-deprivation for soothing when things go badly. After he made a mistake, one man we know would skip breakfast and lunch for days because he felt that he didn't deserve to eat.

Children who are disciplined with spankings or other physical punishments may find that as adults they "accidentally" hurt themselves after they have done something they feel is shameful or wrong. A single woman who was seeing us felt guilty when she reacted to her sister's engagement by feeling angry and jealous rather than joyous. The following day, she "accidentally" dropped a large box on her foot and spent the next week on crutches. She of course had no idea that hurting herself was a way of trying to regain the sense of being worthwhile by re-creating the physical punishments she had received as a child.

To repeat, children are often disciplined for normal behaviors that could better be handled by using loving regulation to keep children and the people or things around them safe or, when appropriate, by simply allowing the behaviors to be outgrown naturally. Babies who reach for the good china or Mom's pearl necklace, toddlers who grab and won't share, three-year-olds who are entirely uninterested in using the toilet, eight-year-olds who stomp off in a huff when they lose a game, and adolescents who forget their chores are all behaving age-appropriately. If these children are, in effect, disciplined for being children, the lesson they learn from their parents' disapproval and punishments is to hold themselves to overly strict standards as adults and then to berate themselves when they fail to measure up. As adults, they are likely to criticize themselves severely for behaviors that others might take in stride. A man who was consulting us felt worthless and painfully depressed because he called someone by the wrong name at a party. A woman was awake all night with insomnia after her boss pointed out one or two grammatical errors on a report she had written.

Adults' problematic behaviors often have their roots in their early relationships with their parents, but they may also have been shaped by experiences with other important adults. Even if you had parents who were strict disciplinarians, the impulse to treat yourself harshly could have been softened if your teachers or other important adults responded to you with understanding and compassion rather than discipline. On the other hand, if the adults you encountered were disciplinarians, your self-critical impulses would have been strengthened. Maybe you can think of times when your teachers or coaches made you feel ashamed or incompetent or times when you were surprised to find that a teacher or coach responded with a kindness you weren't expecting. In either case, those were powerful and influential moments.

Adults who were disciplined as children develop a multitude of ways to treat themselves or others harshly as a way of regaining feelings of being worthwhile when things do not go as they wish. If you are a person who turns on yourself or others when things go wrong, the first step in changing this painful behavior is to understand that unknowingly you are trying to comfort yourself by feeling the way you thought your parents wanted you to feel and by being the person you believed your parents wanted you to be. Strange as it may sound, when you respond to losses by turning on yourself or others, at some level you feel loved and valued. In Section II, Choosing Happiness, we will help you identify and defuse your needs to respond to disappointments and frustrations by becoming a disciplinarian to yourself and others.

## An Addiction to Unhappiness Is Not a Cause for Shame or Self-Blame

The reason we chose the word "addiction" to refer to the learned need for unhappiness is to emphasize that once children confuse unhappiness with happiness, they continue to need some measure of unhappiness to maintain their inner equilibrium. When we refer to someone as having an addiction to unhappiness, we do not mean that the person is morally weak or lacking in will power. Because the addiction to unhappiness occurs before children have a mind that is even close to the mind they will possess as an adult, they have no way to know about this confusion. Nor can they discover it on their own as they grow up. In other words, the addiction to unhappiness is not an intentional choice.

If you find that, like so many people, you have an addiction to unhappiness, there is no reason to feel shame, embarrassment, or disappointment in yourself. By reading these pages you will acquire the tools necessary to turn away from the unhappiness you have mislabeled as happiness and to choose to gratify your inborn thirst for genuine pleasure.

You will learn that there are many different ways in which the addiction to unhappiness can operate outside of your awareness. One common example occurs when people react negatively to the discovery that they have developed a need to make themselves unhappy. If you conclude that you have an addiction to unhappiness and then find yourself feeling embarrassed or self-critical, there is an explanation. Namely, the addiction to unhappiness has seized upon a positive experience (the increasing self-awareness that will give you the tools you need to improve your life) and has given it a negative spin. We help you see that the addiction to unhappiness is not a shameful secret and that knowing about it is the first step toward gaining the ability to choose genuine happiness once and for all. To do this we provide many case examples showing how our clients unknowingly acquired an addiction to unhappiness and how, by recognizing it, they were able to recover and improve their lives.

We cannot overemphasize that when we speak of the addiction to unhappiness we do not mean that you are choosing unhappiness of your own free will. The confusion of unhappiness with happiness and not any failure or weakness on your part is what gives unhappiness its irresistible appeal.

## An Addiction to Unhappiness Does Not Mean Blaming Your Parents

At this point you may be feeling uncomfortable with the notion that your inability to have the life you want is due to mistakes your parents made. This will be especially true if your parents are no longer living or if you have fond memories of your childhood and a close and loving relationship with your parents now. We pause here to emphasize that we are not suggesting that your parents deserve to be blamed for your problems.

There is a crucial distinction between unintentionally causing an injury and being morally responsible for it. You may unknowingly be coming down with the flu and infect everyone in your office, but you are not to blame for their getting ill. Similarly, parents may relate to children in ways that cause them to develop needs to make themselves unhappy, but that doesn't mean that they are blameworthy. In all our years of working with parents, even including abusive parents, we have never met parents who didn't want to do the right thing by their child.

Much child-rearing advice is inaccurate and harmful because it stems from a misunderstanding both of the mind of the newborn and also of the way the child's mind changes and develops from birth through adolescence. Unfortunately, in their attempt to give you the best possible start in life, your parents may have relied on an erroneous notion of what you were really like.

Moreover, your parents were children once, and their notion of good caregiving was to a large extent learned from the parenting they themselves received. Their parents, in turn, reproduced the parenting they received, and so on, for generations back. Using the knowledge you will find here, you can break this pattern and make a fresh start.

There are, of course, parents who are unable to foster their children's inborn happiness because they themselves are beset by emotional difficulties. For example, there are parents whose alcohol addiction or significant mental illness makes it impossible for them to relate in a sufficiently loving, attentive, and appropriate manner to their children.

Other parents who are less dysfunctional are nonetheless made very anxious by some aspect of the parenting process. For example, some parents worry constantly about their children's progress. They hover over them, direct them, and find it hard to let them explore and learn on their own. Their children feel that their own efforts are never good enough. These children often grow up unable to make decisions, or they may go to the opposite extreme and reject any and all advice from others.

There are parents who cannot tolerate their children's unhappiness because it makes them terribly uncomfortable. These parents may keep their children from expressing sadness. ("Don't cry because your toy broke. I'll buy you another.") They may be permissive: that is, they may fail to regulate their children's behavior when required for health and safety reasons because they cannot tolerate their children's unhappiness. For example, they may not insist that their protesting toddler sit in a

car seat on a short trip even though this is necessary to keep the toddler from harm. Children of these parents often develop an addiction
to the false happiness (unhappiness in disguise) of risking their own
safety or the safety of others. When they take chances that would make
most people feel uncomfortable or frightened, they feel satisfied or
exhilarated.

Some parents need to use their children's accomplishments to supply themselves with self-esteem. These parents feel terribly anxious
whenever their children are not first or do not win. One Little League
parent we know fought with an umpire who called his daughter out at
the plate. Children of these parents frequently find it difficult to feel
satisfied with any effort that does not result in a win or an "A."

There are parents who may or may not realize that they need their
children to grow up following in their footsteps. Children of these parents may feel complimented and try to be accommodating, or they may
feel terribly pressured and rebel. In either case they find it almost impossible to experience the genuine pleasure of making their own choices.

### Ron

*Ron's father was an attorney who founded and ran a very lucrative and
successful law firm. From the time Ron was born, his father referred
to him as "a chip off the old block." As Ron grew older, he often told
friends in Ron's presence that he couldn't wait until Ron joined him
in the firm. It never occurred to his father than Ron might not want
to be an attorney. It never occurred to Ron either, until he took a geology course in college and became fascinated with the evolution of land-
masses.*

*Ron took advanced geology courses along with the prelaw curricu-
lum he had been pursuing. The clearer it became to him that he preferred geology, the more guilty he felt. He began to avoid going home,
felt increasingly depressed, and couldn't find the energy to pursue any
goal at all.*

*Finally, Ron went to the student mental health center, where the
guidance counselor pointed out that Ron's assumption that his father*

*would be devastated and disappointed in him for not wanting to be a lawyer was not necessarily accurate. She suggested that Ron speak directly to his father.*

*In a painful state of anxiety, Ron told his father of his dilemma. His father was shocked, of course, and disappointed that his dream was not to be. At the same time, he made absolutely clear to Ron that above all he wanted Ron to pursue a career that would make him happy.*

*Ron was immensely relieved to discover that his fears of ruining his father's life were unfounded. He went on to have a very successful career in geology. His father never tired of talking about his accomplishments.*

This vignette illustrates the powerful effect parents' wishes for their children can have. It also illustrates that the nature of children's minds can prevent them from getting to know the "whole parent." Ron only experienced the part of his father that wanted him to be just like him. As a result, he grew up believing that his father's wishes for him were equivalent to marching orders that he had to follow. He had no way of knowing that when his father was confronted with the reality that Ron wanted to take a different path, he would value Ron's happiness more highly than his own plans for him.

Finally, there are parents who know how to satisfy their children's emotional needs but who are prevented from giving this care as a result of external circumstances. All too often, parents are forced to leave young children due to forces beyond their control, such as social chaos (e.g., war), extreme poverty, unenlightened welfare laws, or serious illness or death. Children are born believing that their parents are all-powerful; therefore, when circumstances beyond parents' control force them to be away from their young children for extended periods of time, children come to an erroneous but natural conclusion. Children conclude that the unhappiness they feel at being left is good because it is what their parents want them to feel and therefore what they should feel, and they become addicted to this unhappiness.

We would like to emphasize the following point: If you have developed an addiction to unhappiness, you can still love and cherish your parents and other important adults even as you recognize that some of their actions were, unintentionally but nonetheless powerfully, the root of your inability to lead the life you want.

*The reason to understand the cause of your need for unhappiness is not to assign blame or to make excuses but to give you the tools you need to take charge of your life and to change it.*

# Chapter 2

# Developing a Need for Relationship Conflict

The addiction to unhappiness can make it difficult to find and to enjoy close friendships and love relationships. Everyone imports from childhood deep-seated assumptions about what makes a good relationship. These assumptions can lead people to:

- Have difficulty making friends or finding partners
- Pick the wrong people as friends and partners and then invest considerable emotional capital in the hopeless effort to make the relationship more rewarding
- Make reasonable choices of friends and partners and then pick fights, lose interest, or otherwise sabotage the relationship they could otherwise enjoy

The good news about the fact that the root of our relationship problems typically lies within us is that we can change ourselves more easily than we can change someone else.

In Chapter 1 we discussed some of the reasons that can cause people periodically, but unknowingly, to need unhappiness. The effects of being left to cry as babies, of having too much expected of them, or of being disciplined, may cause people to need unhappiness and, specifically, affect their ability to enjoy the close, caring relationships everyone desires. They may involve themselves with those who are indifferent to their suffering, who respond harshly when they make mistakes, or who are unavailable or undependable. Or they themselves may find it difficult to be a good friend or partner. For example, they may have trouble being compassionate with friends and partners who are unhappy or who suffer reverses.

In this chapter we are going to discuss other kinds of childhood experiences that can cause people to experience problems finding and enjoying rewarding relationships. The three most important are (1) parents' rejection of children's wishes for closeness and attention, (2) parents' unequal treatment of siblings, and (3) parents' misunderstanding of children's behavior in the Romantic Phase.

As elsewhere, the goal of this discussion is not to assign blame, but to give you the tools you need to improve your life. If an addiction to unhappiness remains invisible to you, it retains the power to sabotage your most fervent resolutions. On the other hand, once this addiction is visible, it can be targeted directly and overcome.

## The Challenge of Becoming Close to Others

Of the many pieces of bad advice your parents may have received, one with especially harmful consequences for your ability to form close, meaningful relationships was the warning that indulging your wishes for closeness and positive attention would make you "too dependent." In our culture *dependence* and *independence* have been wrongly equated with distance from parents. If children wander away from their parents to play, they are erroneously thought of as independent. If they prefer to remain nearby and to play with them, they are mistakenly considered overly dependent and are encouraged to go off and play by themselves. It is normal for children to want to play with their parents at times and to be by themselves at times, but this choice is entirely unrelated to their level of independence.

In reality, all children are born to depend on and to be dependent on their parents. Indeed, the pleasure of being close to parents inspires children to emulate them and to grow up to be caring toward themselves and able to be close to others. The intense attachment you felt for your parents was a developmental achievement, not a sign of weakness. *True independence is not measured by the physical distance between children and parents, but refers to a sustained inner well-being that is independent of external satisfactions and invulnerable to external disappointments.*

True independence is made possible by an inner happiness that does not depend on success and that never crumbles when things don't go as desired. This fundamental well-being arises when parents and important others satisfy young children's intense needs for positive, nurturing attention. This well-being is thwarted by relationship deprivation and distancing.

Around the time of your first birthday, you reached a developmental milestone when you realized that you were happiest if you were in your parents' presence, specifically when you asked for your parents' attention and they responded by being affectionate, by admiring your efforts, or by playing with you. You were passionately attached to them and, for the next two years especially, you needed them to welcome that involvement and to respond positively and enthusiastically. If they had known to do this, you would have developed an optimism about and desire for close relationships that would stand you in good stead today.

On the other hand, if your parents followed popular advice to teach you independence by trying to convince you to tolerate more distance from them just at the time when your needs for involvement were intensifying, you likely melted down and increased your demands for attention. Your parents mistook these demands as indications that you were indeed too dependent and needed to be pushed even farther away. Eventually, you probably concluded that you were wrong to care so much about your parents' interest and approval. You may have tried to feel positively about yourself by pleasing your parents and doing without their attention. If you confused the unhappiness of feeling you shouldn't ask your parents for attention with the happiness of a caring relationship, you would also have developed needs to re-create that unhappiness. Without knowing it, you would have learned lessons that can make it difficult for you to have unruffled positive relationships as an adult and to parent your own children.

### Stan

Stan sought our help because he realized that there was a pattern to his relationships that was causing him much unhappiness and frustration. He would fall in love with a woman and pursue her wholeheartedly. He would send her flowers, take her to nice restaurants, and call her two or three times a day. But the moment that the woman he was wooing began to reciprocate his affections, Stan began to lose interest in her. If a woman made clear that she was crazy about him and wanted to spend as much time as possible with him, Stan felt suffocated. This feeling was unpleasant and he began to dislike the woman for being so "dependent" on him and "causing" him to feel so much discomfort. Next he would stop calling her and begin looking for someone new.

When we began working with Stan he complained bitterly that it was impossible to find a woman who was "independent." He said, "No matter how independent women seem at first, as time goes by they all become clingy and demanding." Stan's distorted idea of independence, a quality he highly valued, was that it was virtuous never to want or need involvement with anyone else. He felt much more comfortable choosing the false pleasure of isolation over the genuine pleasure of closeness and mutuality.

Stan was astonished to hear that healthy involvement with others brought with it feelings of needing and wanting to be with those others. He said, "I remember so many times when as a child I begged my parents to play with me, but they refused, saying I should act like a 'big boy.' They wouldn't grant any of my wishes until I asked in a way that did not seem so intense and 'babyish.' And they really liked it when I played by myself and didn't ask for any attention." Stan had tried hard to fulfill his parents' desire that he be more "independent" and "grown-up" and had felt proud and close to his parents whenever he could stop himself from requesting their attention or affection.

As Stan's involvement in the therapeutic relationship deepened, he found himself looking forward to his next session. He reacted by feeling angry at himself for becoming so "dependent" on our relationship. He skipped sessions to show himself that he could do without us. Over time, he realized that his feelings of needing and wanting to see us were healthy and normal rather than shameful and unmanly, and eventually he was able to apply this new understanding to the romantic relationships in his life. He met and courted Susan, and when he began to dislike her for "expecting too much" of him, instead of breaking up with her immediately, he turned to us for help evaluating those feelings.

The most important change in Stan was that he now doubted his old assumptions about the qualities of a good relationship. Instead of confusing the false pleasure of remaining aloof with real happiness, he began to seek closeness and genuine involvement. He restrained himself from voicing the feelings of dislike he felt for Susan when she wanted to spend more time together. As time passed, Stan became able both to enjoy and to feel gratified by Susan's expressions of affection, and also to let himself accept his growing attachment to her and the accompanying feelings of wanting to be with her.

Sometimes people whose addiction to unhappiness makes it difficult to create and sustain close relationships *consciously* pursue, desire, and prize involvement, but they unknowingly satisfy their need to re-create the relationship distance they experienced with their parents by repeatedly choosing partners who cannot tolerate commitment.

### Nancy

Nancy, an account executive in her twenties, made every possible effort to meet the man of her dreams. She wanted nothing so much as to get married and start a family. She told all of her friends that she was "in the market," and she joined biking and hiking clubs, which had a high ratio of men to women. Time after time, she would meet someone who seemed nice; they would go out a few times; she would enjoy his company and look forward to getting more involved. But just as the relationship began to become more intense, the man would stop calling. Nancy would overlook this negative signal and continue to call him and suggest that they spend time together. When he either didn't return her calls or repeatedly said he was busy, she had to face the fact that he was no longer interested in her. As these painful experiences multiplied, Nancy began to feel increasingly discouraged and cynical. She hesitated to begin new relationships and withdrew from most of her social activities. Finally, at a friend's suggestion, she consulted us.

When we suggested that, without realizing it, Nancy was choosing men who were frightened of involvement, she doubted that this was possible. She said, "There is no way anyone can know this when they first meet someone." She pointed to the lengths to which she had gone to meet someone who wanted a long-term relationship, and she argued that most men are "just like that." At the same time, she did acknowledge that there seemed to be no variation in the type of man that attracted her—every one disappeared when the relationship began to intensify.

As Nancy reflected on her own life, she realized how affected she had been by the fact that her own father had been a workaholic who was rarely home. When she would beg him to come to a school play or ask him to take her and her friends to a movie, he would reply that he was too busy—that "someone has to make the money around here." Moreover, she could never remember a time when her father had spontaneously hugged or kissed her. In fact, he had always seemed uncomfortable when she showed him any affection.

Nancy began to understand that, like all of us, she was tremendously affected by a parent's attitude toward closeness. While consciously she sought a committed intimate relationship, at the same time she had accepted her father's standoffishness as justified and had condemned her own longings for his attention as inappropriate and childish. Without realizing it, she solved this conflict by picking men whose attraction was that they felt familiar—that is, their emotional distance reminded her of her father. It was not surprising, then, that these men left at the first sign of real involvement.

Nancy's difficulties with relationships began to surface in the treatment relationship with us. On the one hand, she was pleased that the therapeutic relationship was so stable and helpful. On the other hand, her addiction to unhappiness caused her to feel uncomfortable with her positive involvement with us. Like Stan, she accused us of making her "dependent." These negative feelings surprised her and alerted her to the possibility that she might in fact have been instinctively avoiding men who were ready and available for a close committed relationship.

As time went on, Nancy made an effort to override her instincts about whom to date, which she now knew to be faulty, and to get to know men who asked her out but whom she would not previously have considered. To her surprise, some of them turned out to be enjoyable and interesting and, most important, they did not all run at the first sign of involvement.

Nancy made the important discovery that when she dated a man who remained interested in her, she began to lose interest in him. We encouraged her not to act on those feelings until our work together clarified whether her lack of interest in the relationship reflected her learned dislike of closeness or a genuine perception that the other person was not right for her. When Nancy found that she could not think of anything really "wrong" with the man she was seeing, she admitted to herself that she must have the same conflict about closeness that had upset her so much in the men she previously dated.

This was a turning point in Nancy's work with us. Shortly afterward, she began to enjoy and appreciate the close relationship that was developing between herself and her current partner.

Sometimes the unrecognized need to sabotage the pleasure of closeness with another doesn't show up until after a real commitment has been made. It is not uncommon for people who are convinced they are marrying their true love to wake up the morning after their wedding feeling trapped and wondering what they ever saw in their spouse. If they don't realize that these negative feelings are expressions of the addiction to unhappiness, the marriage may be destroyed.

### Jim

Jim came to see us because his wife had asked for a divorce. As we talked with him, it became clear that he loved his wife and wanted to stay married to her. Yet from the day they got married he felt he had been happiest when they had simply lived together as roommates. Although before their marriage they had had a reasonably satisfying sex life, now when his wife wanted affection Jim mostly felt claustrophobic and disapproving toward her. Frustrated by what she experienced as a loveless marriage, Jim's wife told him to leave. Jim wanted to save his marriage, but he also felt very angry at his wife for being so "demanding and needy."

As Jim became comfortable confiding in us, he increasingly shared his confusion about his wife's needs for affection. He felt that he had showed her how much he loved and cared about her by marrying her and that it was unreasonable of her to demand that he keep "proving" his love by being physically affectionate.

When we asked him to tell us more about these feelings, Jim told us that he just felt more comfortable when he kept a certain distance from other people, including his wife. As a child, he remembered being praised by his parents for his ability to play for long periods without needing attention. He also recalled that on the rare occasions when he asked his parents for help with a problem, they would insist that he try harder to solve it on his own. The moment that he learned to read, his parents stopped reading to him. Moreover, from the age of four, when Jim wanted to sit in his parents' laps he was told that he was too old. He remembered feeling proud on the many occasions that his parents told their friends what a self-sufficient boy he was.

From his birth Jim's parents seem to have been uncomfortable with Jim's healthy needs for love and affection. In the course of emulating *his parents' rejection of his needs for closeness, Jim unknowingly developed a deep conviction that isolation from others was a sign of strength and would make him happy, whereas needs for affection were a sign of weakness. At the same time, of course, he retained the longing for close, positive relationships with which he was born.*

*Once Jim realized that his wishes to have a healthy marriage were being thwarted by his discomfort with closeness and interdependence, Jim was inspired to pursue the relationship pleasure he had previously scorned. He approached his wife and asked her to hold off on the divorce. He promised to do everything possible to become a husband who could make her happy. Much to his relief, his wife agreed to wait while he continued to work with us.*

In summary, if you find that you are uncomfortable because you are feeling "too involved" with a friend or partner, or if you habitually seem to choose partners who are aloof, who run at the first sign of closeness, or who refuse to give up "playing the field" even though they are romantically involved with you, without realizing it you are perpetuating negative feelings about closeness that you learned in childhood. When your parents worried about giving you too much affection, you came to feel good about yourself when you kept your distance from others. Of course, as a child you had no way to know that your parents and other important adults were engaged in a misguided effort to make you independent and that they never would have wanted to damage your ability to enjoy close relationships as an adult. Fortunately, it is not too late to change these negative assumptions about involvement and to learn to enjoy intimate friendships and love relationships.

## The Struggle to Feel Secure in Relationships

Without realizing it, parents often give their children the message that they prefer one to the others, that they think more highly of one than of the others, or that they dislike one. Sometimes the favoritism divides along gender lines. A father may devote hours to throwing a baseball with his son, but be unwilling to make the same investment in a daughter who enjoys playing "catch." A mother may spend a lot of time cooking and chatting with a daughter, but be reluctant to take the time to teach her son to cook. Sometimes one child will remind a parent of a favorite aunt or a hated stepsister and the child will be favored or disliked accordingly. In some families parents feel particularly proud of a child they believe to be unusually intelligent, and they are disappointed in siblings who don't seem as smart. Birth order sometimes affects parents, who may feel most involved with their first child or fondest of their youngest offspring.

When parents discriminate among siblings in this way, children confuse the unhappiness they feel at being liked or disliked for specific attributes with the true happiness that comes from being loved for themselves alone, and they develop needs to re-create some form of this unhappiness later in life. Moreover, they learn that there is not enough parental love to go around and they adopt the view that relationships are competitions for scarce resources. As children they learn to view their siblings as competitors, and they carry this attitude into adulthood. They conceive of friendships and other relationships as struggles for affection.

### Simone

*Simone was the youngest of three sisters and a strikingly beautiful child. Her mother, who had never thought of herself as attractive, was thrilled to have given birth to such a gorgeous girl. Without meaning to discriminate, she always bought Simone the most expensive clothes and spent the most time brushing and styling her hair. Simone was delighted to be her mother's favorite. She never knew, of course, that her feelings of being special really represented the unhappiness of being admired for her looks rather than for the person she was.*

*As an adult, Simone continued to be addicted to this disguised form of unhappiness. She overspent on clothes and makeup, and she constantly solicited compliments on her appearance. It was very difficult for Simone to make good friends. She only chose friends whose looks couldn't compete with hers and then couldn't restrain herself from constantly asking for their admiration.*

*The process of aging finally brought Simone in to see us. No matter how much cosmetic surgery she had or how much money she spent on clothes, she no longer received the compliments and attention from men that had been showered on her when she was younger. Her addiction to the false happiness produced by her good looks was going unsatisfied, and she became quite depressed.*

*We worked with Simone for a long time before she was able to get over her need for constant feedback on her beauty. For months she would dress up for her appointments with us only to become upset and convinced we didn't care about her when we didn't mention her appearance. As we continued to try to be of help during the many sessions in which she felt angry and frustrated with us, Simone began to realize that there are other, more satisfying ways to be cared about. Gradually she focused less on her appearance and began to look around for more meaningful sources of pleasure. She discovered that she really enjoyed working with clay. While taking a pottery course, she made friends with fellow students whose companionship she enjoyed. Weeks later, she felt pleased when she realized that she had never once thought to compare their looks to hers.*

As adults, children whose parents compare them unfavorably to their siblings may find themselves compensating by seeking the false happiness produced by being the object of admiration. They assume without realizing it that their siblings were happy because they were preferred, and they turn every relationship into a quest for praise. This single-minded determination to win admiration can make their relationships one-sided and difficult.

Sometimes siblings who are not favored develop needs for the pain of feeling inferior, which they have confused with happiness by supposing it is what they are meant to feel. As adults they seek out situations in which others are more successful and more admired, and they take care never to stand out in a crowd. They create relationships with partners to whom they feel inferior. This satisfies the addiction to unhappiness, but it leaves their inborn desire for genuine happiness and positive relationships unfulfilled.

In general, when siblings are valued unequally by their parents, as adults they choose relationships in which they re-create the jealous, competitive, superior, or inferior feelings that filled their childhoods. They unknowingly conclude that these feelings are good because, like all children, they believe that whatever they feel, no matter how unpleasant, is desirable because it is what their perfect parents mean for them to experience.

## The Romantic Family Drama

If your dissatisfaction with your life results to any extent from the lack of meaningful relationships or from unrewarding relationships, one major cause may be found in the childhood period we call *the romantic phase,* which spans roughly the years from three to six. Child development researchers have long recognized that at about the age of three children begin preferentially to seek the attentions of the opposite-sex parent. Children not only entertain diffuse wishes for a special and exclusive relationship with the opposite-sex parent, but also experience reactive fears that the same-sex parent will be angry with them for wanting to take the same-sex parent's place. These wishes and fears explain much puzzling behavior, such as ongoing, intense competitiveness; moodiness; extreme sensitivity to "slights;" and assertions of superhuman powers and perfect knowledge.

When parents do not understand the dynamics of this phase, they may find much of children's behavior incomprehensible or, worse, blameworthy. This is an emotionally intense period and children at this age are very sensitive. Depending on the way the romantic phase is handled by parents it can either facilitate an adult's ability to form positive, meaningful relationships or cause an adult to be addicted to conflicted and unhappy relationships.

We emphasize that children in the romantic phase are not pursuing a fully adult relationship with the opposite-sex parent, but are imitating the social relationship they perceive their parents to have. Children have a very nonspecific idea of their parents' romantic relationship. This notion includes elements of romantic possessiveness, affection, and exclusivity. Children in the romantic phase are not seeking any type of sexualized attention or contact. Tragically, sex offenders' gross misinterpretation of children's behavior in this phase as being romantic in an adult sense sometimes causes them to argue that their child victims seduced them.

About the time children turn three, they begin to realize that their parents have a relationship with each other that doesn't include them, and they want in on this newly recognized source of fun. (We will discuss situations in which a parent is absent or parents don't get along with each other. For now, we are discussing children whose parents enjoy each other's company.) Children want to have the opposite-sex parent to themselves and to get the same positive attention the same-sex parent is getting. They don't understand the exact nature of their parents' relationship, but they know they want to deflect the opposite-sex parent's admiration in their direction. To illustrate, when the mother of a little boy, Greg, complimented her husband on his singing, Greg immediately began singing at the top of his voice.

Parents who understand that this intense desire for admiration is normal will feel free to praise the most off-key effort. They might say to Greg, "You have a terrific voice. Would you like to sing another song?"

Parents who are following popular advice to keep children from feeling "too full of themselves," tend to respond negatively. They say something like, "Greg, you have to learn that you can't always be the center of attention and that you can't be the best at everything." Children who are criticized or teased for their wish to be admired by the opposite-sex parent typically respond by feeling ashamed and inhibited. They may stop trying to get positive attention from members of the opposite sex. As adults they may feel most comfortable giving others all the credit for their efforts. Perhaps the most famous example is the character of Cyrano de Bergerac. Believing himself too unattractive to be loved for himself, Cyrano helped another man to woo the woman he loved.

Sometimes children who are criticized or teased for their attempts to be admired cling to these wishes and redouble their efforts. As adults, they may unintentionally alienate others by their constant need for praise and admiration.

The reason that children between three and six are able to believe that they are realistic competitors for the opposite-sex parent's attention is that the immaturity of their minds prevents them from understanding the nature of their parents' commitment to each other. Children also have an unrealistic self-image, which overshadows the differences in intellectual maturity and physical size and power between children and their parents. One little boy proclaimed that he was a better basketball player than Michael Jordan. When he shot and missed, he looked at his parents in disgust and said, "The basket is broken."

Like other children, you probably announced frequently that you were stronger and knew more than your parents, especially the parent of the same sex. If your parents understood that this overvaluation of your abilities was both normal and temporary, they were able to react affectionately and acceptingly. When five-year-old Bobby announced that he was a much faster runner than his father, his Dad responded, "Wow, that's terrific!" He knew that Bobby's response was age-appropriate and that his son would outgrow this unrealistic view of himself more completely and without emotional scars if he did not attempt to puncture Bobby's illusions.

On the other hand, when parents regularly respond to their children's assertion of superior powers and abilities with ridicule, irritation, teasing, criticism, or factual corrections, children feel hurt and deflated. They begin to doubt their ability to get the most important people in their world to give them the admiration they so desperately seek. As adults, they may cling to unrealistic views of their own abilities, may be unable to feel proud of their most successful efforts, or may be unable to tolerate constructive criticism. Moreover, they may copy what they experienced as their parents' unwillingness to satisfy their needs for recognition and have great difficulty complimenting others.

### Mike

*Mike, a salesman for a printing company, came to us because he was in danger of losing his job for the third time in two years. He said that he knew he was too "thin skinned." He thrived on compliments, which made him feel on top of the world, and he would fish for them at every opportunity. By taking all the credit, he irritated customers who worked with him on designs for brochures and catalogs. At the same time, Mike couldn't tolerate even a hint of constructive criticism. If his boss or a customer suggested that he could improve in some area, he would defend himself vigorously and blame others for the problem.*

*Mike imported the same sensitivities into the therapeutic relationship with us. He took the slightest indication from us that he might be getting in his own way as criticism that had to be disproved. He accused us of being just like his father, who he said was quick to find fault with him and hardly ever gave him credit for a good effort. As Mike talked about his childhood, it became clear that his father had not understood his son's need to feel on an equal footing with him during the romantic phase. His father saw his young son's competitiveness and extravagant claims for his own powers as dangerous traits that had to be stamped out. He frequently told the child that he "needed to be taken down a peg." Mike had many memories of his father saying, "You aren't nearly as good as you think you are."*

*We learned not to assume that Mike could tolerate our input. We waited until he felt up to asking what we thought before offering an opinion. Very slowly, Mike realized that we were on his side, trying to help. He started to believe that our observations about how unhappy he was making himself came from a positive wish to be of assistance rather than from a motive to diminish him. As he became less driven to reject our help, Mike discovered that he was his own worst critic. Consciously he felt angry at the way his father had criticized him. But as is the case with all children, deep down he equated being like his father with being loved by him. In this instance, the result was that Mike had adopted a harsh and unforgiving attitude toward himself. It was no wonder that he was so sensitive to constructive criticism, which he experienced as a confirmation of his worst fears about himself. At the same time, even though it caused him to feel much emotional pain, Mike's self-criticism had the meaning of being like his father and, therefore, of being loved by his father and able to feel positively about himself.*

*As Mike worked with us, his need to use self-criticism to maintain his inner equilibrium diminished, while his inner well-being increasingly was nourished by constructive thoughts and feelings about himself. As a result, Mike became more able to tolerate suggestions from others. While constructive criticism from his boss or his customers still caused him difficulty, he was much more able to assume that it arose in wishes to help him to do his job better. He refrained from arguing and tried to implement the suggestions. He gradually felt secure enough to compliment a customer who contributed a good idea. His job performance and his enjoyment of his work improved greatly.*

Another aspect of the romantic phase that can have long term effects on adult relationships is the child's fear that the same-sex parent will retaliate in response to the child's competitive wishes. Because children are convinced that they are more appealing than the same-sex parent, when the opposite-sex parent does not respond to their romantic wishes, children inevitably conclude that the problem is interference by the same-sex parent. This is the reason that children in this phase are so often angry and rejecting of the same-sex parent and, in turn, why they are so fearful that the same-sex parent will react with matching anger and rejection.

Although they will accompany the opposite-sex parent on the most tedious errand, children of this age often will not even play games they like with the same-sex parent. Same-sex parents who don't understand this phase and the extent of children's vulnerability may feel hurt by children's rejection and express that hurt in ways that are very upsetting to children who are already worried that their anger will cause the same-sex parent to retaliate. For example, when their child rejects an offer to spend time together, same-sex parents who don't understand this phase frequently say something like, "Well then, I don't want to play with you either. I would rather read my paper." Children in this stage need a lot of reassurance. When same-sex parents communicate feeling hurt, rejected, or angry, this only confirms children's fears. As adults, children who are responded to in this way may destroy close relationships by turning the expectation of rejection by friends and partners into a self-fulfilling prophecy.

### Ellen

*Ellen was a graduate student in her early twenties who sought our help because her close friendships were so turbulent. She had no trouble making friends, but immediately thereafter conflict would break out. Ellen would begin to doubt the friend's loyalty and commitment to her. If the friend made plans with another friend or began to date someone, Ellen concluded that the friend didn't like her and didn't want to be with her. Ellen would react by becoming cool and distant. The friend, naturally, would respond to Ellen's unfriendliness with anger or withdrawal, thereby confirming Ellen's worst suspicions.*

*Ellen recalled that while her relationships with men had always been satisfactory, she had never had a smooth relationship with a woman. She said that she had had a turbulent time with her own mother. She had been a "Daddy's girl" and her mother had always resented the closeness Ellen shared with her father. Her mother made clear that she felt hurt when Ellen would confide in her father but not in her. Ellen accepted her mother's complaints as the price she had to pay for the enjoyable times with her father.*

*As Ellen got more involved in her treatment, she found herself resenting the other people who came to us. She also accused us of caring more about others than we did about her. She was convinced that we had "favorites" and bitterly concluded that she was not one of them.*

*As gently as possible, we pointed out that Ellen had adopted her mother's view of relationships as competitions for a limited amount of positive attention. At first Ellen was outraged by the notion that she possessed qualities that she had so disliked in her mother, but we helped her to realize that as a child the only way she had had of feeling close to her mother had been to become like her in some ways.*

*Over time, Ellen perceived that we remained attentive and caring toward her in spite of her anger at us and the fact that we saw other clients. Slowly she began to think of relationships as opportunities for constructive pleasure rather than as a struggle for favors and attention. Her attitude toward her women friends became less possessive and more confident, with the result that her friends enjoyed her company more and included her more often.*

Opposite-sex parents who do not understand the romantic phase may react to their young child's preference for them with disapproval or irritation. The opposite-sex parent may feel uncomfortable with the child's intense affection and may feel sorry for the same-sex parent. In response, the opposite-sex parent may refuse to honor the child's preference and insist that the child be read to, put to bed, or played with by the same-sex parent. Children who receive this sort of rebuff to their intense wishes to spend time with the opposite-sex parent may grow up inhibited and shy toward members of the opposite sex.

## The Romantic Phase: A Blueprint for Today's Relationships

The romantic phase culminates in the *relationship ideal*, an identification with the way your parents treated you, each other, friends, and strangers. An identification is the attempt to be just like people who are important to us. It is a blueprint for how we act as adults. This is one reason the romantic phase has such a powerful effect on your current relationships.

When parents know that the child's preference for the opposite-sex parent is normal at this age and that children will outgrow it on their own, they can usually take it in stride. When children see that the same-sex parent does not retaliate as expected, they discover a model of relating that includes the ability to remain close to loved ones who have different opinions and wishes.

If the romantic phase goes as it should, children recognize that the disappointment they feel when they don't succeed in displacing the same-sex parent in the eyes of the opposite-sex parent is not due to their own shortcomings or to any defect in their parents' love for them, but to the committed love their parents feel for each other. Children become increasingly realistic about their own powers when they realize that although they can get their parents to care for and about them, they cannot dictate the manner in which their parents lead their personal lives. This recognition allows children to make the crucial perception that they will be happier basking in the warmth of the parent–child relationship than pursuing the unsatisfying course of trying to interfere with their parents' romantic relationships. As adults, these children will not pursue emotionally unavailable partners or get themselves into messy friendships or love triangles.

Children whose parents are divorced or dislike each other may develop ideals of relating that cause them problems as adults. For example, if the same-sex parent is absent or disliked by the opposite-sex parent, and the opposite-sex parent reacts by showering excessive attention on the child, the child may feel victorious over the same-sex parent. These children may grow up believing that relationship pleasure is generated by struggling for a prize and then winning it.

### Roger

Roger was a 40-year-old successful architect who had a turbulent personal life. He satisfied his needs for romance by pursuing women who were involved with other men. If the woman left the other man for him, Roger would gradually lose interest in her and the cycle would begin again. Two or three times, Roger had been unable to stop himself from wooing women who were dating friends of his. At the time he convinced himself that the women were worth the loss of the friendship because he was madly in love. The result was that he lost dear friends and then lost interest in the women as well.

When Roger began to feel an irresistible temptation to pursue the girlfriend of a senior partner in his firm, he realized that he was about to jeopardize his job and he immediately consulted us. Roger's parents had divorced when he was five. Roger remembered his mother saying to him, "You're the man in the house now—you're the one I have to depend on." His mother frequently asked him how he liked different outfits that she would wear and consulted him about plans to redecorate their apartment. Roger had felt proud and pleased at being so valued. He also remembered that shouldering the responsibility to keep his mother's spirits up sometimes made him feel stifled and overwhelmed. In high school he would often stay out late many nights in a row in order to avoid going home.

Roger's relationship with his father had been equally conflicted. On the one hand, he recalled feeling superior to his father because his mother had preferred Roger in the role of man of the house. But he also remembered longing for his father to come back and relieve him of some of the responsibility for his mother's well-being.

Roger had never connected his childhood experiences with his drive to take women away from other men and his subsequent inability to sustain his romantic interest in a woman once she was "his." Roger told us, "I guess I have always thought of love as a contest in which there are only winners and losers." Gradually he began to see that a good relationship is about enjoying the other person rather than winning her away from someone else.

With our help Roger struggled mightily and largely successfully with his impulse to flirt with women who were involved with other men. At first he complained that there wasn't one unattached woman who interested him. We pointed out that the lack of excitement he felt probably meant that he was missing the familiar (though false) pleasure of victory over a third party. He had become addicted to that feeling of triumph, which is really a pain-ridden type of pleasure that is unrelated to loving another person. He had been pursuing women not because he was truly interested in them but because winning them made him feel successful and powerful.

After some time, Roger met an unattached woman who interested him. Our work with Roger now focused on helping him to enjoy this new way of relating.

When the romantic phase goes well, children are left with a solid, constructive model of how to interact with friends, children, and loved ones. They copy parents who love each other while preserving their commitment to care appropriately for their child. This blueprint allows children to grow up to have meaningful relationships that remain close and unthreatened in the face of differences of opinion or conflicting preferences. Because as children their anger did not jeopardize their relationship with the same-sex parent, as adults they are not afraid to hear or express disagreement. Because as children they continued to get abundant parenting attention from the opposite-sex parent even when that parent didn't give them the social attention they desired, as adults they do not feel hurt or rejected if a friend or partner has interests or opinions they do not share.

When the romantic phase does not go well, children are left with a model of relating that will intensify their addiction to unhappiness and cause them problems finding and preserving close relationships as adults. This model may incline them to become excessively jealous, possessive, or competitive, or to become impatient with others who have a different perspective or who make different choices.

In sum, you will be on your way to improving your relationships if you pause to identify the model for relating that you imported from your childhood. Ask yourself these questions: Do you see friendships as competitions for a limited quantity of pleasure? Do feelings of jealousy make every relationship painful? Do you have a difficult time preserving close feelings with friends or partners who make everyday choices (what movie to see, where to go on vacation) that wouldn't be your choices? Are you most attracted by people who are emotionally unavailable? Do you seem to choose friends and partners who tend to dominate or criticize you? Do you seem to choose friends and partners whom you dominate or devalue? Do you lose interest in or pick fights with friends and partners who show a great interest in you? Do you need the other to feel like a complete person?

If the answer to any of these questions is "Yes," then your model for relationships needs reworking. In Section 2 we will show you how to attain satisfying and lasting relationships that do not partake of the negative assumptions about relating that you learned as a child.

## Beyond Your Parents

In this and the preceding chapter we have described the nature and causes of the addiction to unhappiness. Before we look in more detail at the consequences of being addicted to unhappiness, we would like to pause and address a question we know many of our readers will want to ask: How can it be that so much of the way we are is established at such an early age—what about the effect of all the people we meet and the experiences we have later on?

The parenting an individual receives early in life is the most powerful influence, positive or negative, on that individual's emotional health for two reasons: (1) children are born loving their parents, believing their parents are perfect, and needing to imitate them; and (2) early in life children's minds are sufficiently immature that they cannot evaluate the quality of the care they receive.

The inner equilibrium of people who possess an unshakable inner well-being and an appetite solely for constructive pleasure cannot be affected by people and events encountered in later childhood and in adulthood. In contrast, life experiences can positively or negatively impact the quality of life of individuals who have developed an addiction to unhappiness. Because these individuals' needs for inner well-being can be met either by genuine pleasure or by unhappiness masquerading as genuine pleasure, other people and events can influence whether these individuals turn to happiness or unhappiness to maintain their inner equilibrium. Positive experiences, such as having good fortune, encountering kind and caring teachers and bosses, and growing up in a benign peer culture are likely to strengthen these individuals' desires to satisfy their emotional needs with genuine, constructive pleasure. Negative experiences, such as being the target of racism or sexism, having peers who regularly break the law, being dominated by tyrannical teachers (or, later, unfair bosses), or encountering really bad luck will tend to strengthen these individuals' tendencies to turn to unhappiness to supply themselves with inner well-being.

If you have an addiction to unhappiness, the insights, guidelines, and strategies you will find here will give you the tools to change the balance between positive and negative ways of supplying yourself with inner well-being. Whereas previously you may have felt helpless when you couldn't follow through on a resolution, now you know that in reality at those moments you were actively, though unknowingly, comforting yourself with a painful experience. You will learn how to turn away from pain masquerading as pleasure and how to choose constructive pleasure as your source of deepest well-being.

# Chapter 3

# Self-Sabotage: The Unhappiness Fix

If you are addicted to unhappiness, the effects can reverberate through your everyday experience in ways that you may or may not recognize. They can cause disturbances in your moods, in your desire to stay fit and healthy, in your wish to maintain and enjoy close relationships, and in your determination to succeed at your chosen career. Before you can take the steps necessary to conquer this addiction and take charge of your own life, you need to be aware of how it is affecting you. This chapter is a general introduction to the ways the addiction to unhappiness can undermine your pursuit of genuine pleasure and prevent you from having the life you want. This self-sabotage may occur in any part of your life. In Section II we offer practical strategies for overcoming the addiction to unhappiness in specific areas of your life.

The addiction to unhappiness may affect you in four main ways:

- *Your well-being may be dependent on external events.* You may find it difficult to shake off disappointments, you may measure your inner worth by your outward successes, or you may evaluate yourself through the eyes of others. The forms this disequilibrium takes may vary, but the result is the same: when things go wrong, they often go doubly wrong. There is the disappointment itself and also the loss of self-esteem that it frequently stimulates.

- *You may find that without knowing it you sometimes pursue painful experiences rather than genuine pleasure.* You may experience frequent bouts of painful feelings, such as depression, or unfounded fears. You may pick the wrong people as friends and lovers or you may find it difficult to experience closeness and mutuality with the right people. You may find it difficult to maintain good health and general physical well-being. You may have chosen a career that doesn't suit your talents or you may find it difficult to succeed at a career you really enjoy.
- *Experiences of genuine happiness may arouse unrecognized needs for unhappiness.* You may subtly undermine positive efforts you are making toward goals you have set at work, in relationships, or for your health. When you achieve a goal you have long sought, you may experience unaccountable periods of depression, self-criticism, and anxiety that you don't realize are reactions to your success. You may reach a goal and then do something to ruin your achievement.
- *Often the addiction to unhappiness shows itself as difficulty regulating the need for certain pleasures. Many people who otherwise feel in charge of their lives struggle to control their eating, drinking, hours spent working, and sexual appetitie.*

## True Security Comes from Within

If you were left to cry as a baby or punished or disapproved of for behaving like a child, you probably periodically felt unworthy of your parents' love. You would unknowingly have been comfortable (happy) feeling unhappy because you would have believed it was the way your parents wanted you to feel and, therefore, the way you should feel. You would also have developed needs to re-create that disguised unhappiness by feeling unworthy. At the same time, though, you would have retained your inborn wish for the type of happiness that is generated by positive rather than negative experiences. To gratify that wish, you most likely turned to external sources of well-being, such as getting what you wanted when you wanted it, or the approval of others. To this day, your inner equilibrium may still rest on externals, which makes it inherently vulnerable to disruption.

## Dealing with Disappointment

If your emotional well-being depends on externals, you lack an emotional safety net to catch you when things go wrong. The losses that throw off your inner equilibrium may be as minor as losing a pen or being unable to get concert tickets you want, or they may be as significant as the illness of a loved one or the loss of a job. We emphasize that we are not referring here to the sadness everyone feels at disappointments or significant bad luck. In the presence of an addiction to unhappiness, appropriate sadness due to everyday losses is often compounded when people turn for comfort to feelings of worthlessness, shame, or anger at themselves or those around them.

Babies and young children who don't receive consistent comforting find it difficult to comfort themselves in constructive ways when they feel unhappy. They copy what they understand to be reluctance on the part of those in charge to help them feel better and they feel good about themselves when they forgo the soothing they desire. As we explained earlier, in reality your parents did want to make you genuinely happy. But *like all children, your beliefs about your parents' intentions came entirely from the effects their actions had on the way you felt.*

All parents get irritable and exhausted at times. If your parents were occasionally cranky or unresponsive, your emotional development would not have been affected because these moments would have been exceptions in an overall atmosphere of attentiveness to your needs. But if, with the best intentions in the world, your parents frequently let you cry without trying to soothe your tears, responded negatively to your wishes to be close to them and to have their attention, expected more maturity than you were capable of as a child, disciplined you, or were permissive (didn't protect you from the consequences of your immaturity), you concluded that the uncomforted misery you felt was good because it was the result of your parents' love. You developed needs to recapture that familiar feeling (of misery) by re-creating it for yourself.

Children whose parents regularly isolate them or disapprove of them when they are unhappy do feel sad and bad and even angry, but underneath they are certain that their parents are giving them ideal love. Without realizing it, they mistake the pain of going uncomforted for the deep pleasure of being completely loved by perfect parents and, as adults, they try to comfort themselves by re-creating sad, upset, and uncomforted feelings. This is why so many people are unable to shake off disappointments. The pain of an actual loss is compounded by the unrecognized tendency to seek comfort by feeling ashamed, unlovable, guilty, enraged, or victimized.

If you frequently went uncomforted as a child, as an adult you may find yourself struggling internally when things do not go well in the outside world. If you lose a hard-fought tennis match or if a report you worked hard on is largely ignored, you may have difficulty maintaining your inner equilibrium. You suffer the loss itself and then you also suffer from the sad, bad, or angry feelings that you turn to as a way of soothing the disappointment you feel.

### Carl

*Every time a sale he was pursuing fell through, Carl felt worthless and painfully depressed. Even though rationally Carl knew that a certain number of sales never work out, his miserable feelings were so strong that many days passed before he felt able to make more cold calls. As a result, his job was seriously jeopardized.*

*After we had worked with Carl for a period of time, he began to see that the self-hatred he felt was completely out of proportion to losing a sale. He remembered, "As a child I felt so mortified by mistakes that I tried my best to avoid situations in which I was likely to make them.*

*In high school I never wanted to take the advanced placement classes for which I was eligible. I always took easier courses instead."*

Carl had many memories of being punished for errors. For example, he remembered a time when as a six-year-old he accidentally dropped a platter he was drying. He was called clumsy and careless and made to pay for a new platter with weeks of his allowance. While he had hated losing his allowance, he had never questioned the principle that he should pay for his mistake.

These memories helped Carl to see that when things went wrong he had been unknowingly soothing himself with the unhappiness he felt when he copied his parents and made himself "pay." Previously he had hardly even noticed his self-critical responses because they felt deserved and, therefore, appropriate. He now realized that his parents, with whom he presently had a close relationship, did not want him to grow up paralyzed by mistakes and recognized that their negative responses had been based on their erroneous belief that his slips had been negligent or willful.

Carl increasingly recognized that he had to work harder than his friends and colleagues to stay on an even keel when things went wrong. Moreover, it took him a long time to believe that we were not angry or disappointed in him when he lost a sale. Eventually, his newfound determination to be kinder to himself grew in strength, while the attraction of soothing himself with self-criticism waned. He still felt disappointed when he lost a sale, but he could usually maintain his sense of inner balance, of being a loveable and worthwhile person. As a result, he no longer found it so difficult to make the next call.

If you sometimes turn on yourself when things do not go well, knowing the reason why is the first step toward eliminating this unnecessary pain. If you apply for a job you want and don't get it, you will certainly feel disappointed. If you are aware that you are likely to react to that disappointment by becoming depressed, feeling worthless, and losing the self-confidence you need to apply for other jobs, you can begin to see that these unpleasant feelings are your attempt to comfort yourself the way you were "soothed" as a child. This knowledge is the leverage you need to cease making yourself doubly unhappy when things do not turn out as you wish.

## Success Is Not a Good Measure of Self-Worth

If you left childhood feeling insecure about whether you were loveable and loved, chances are that you regularly use success as a measure of your self-worth. These successes may be as significant as a big promotion at work or as minor as winning a card game. With so much at stake emotionally, winning can become so important that it is impossible to feel satisfied with a good effort that doesn't succeed. Moreover, an intensely competitive outlook driven by the fear of how devastated you will feel if you don't win can make it difficult to maintain smooth relationships with friends and coworkers.

### Jeff
*Jeff was an air traffic controller who played golf "to relax." However his mood fluctuated with the score on every hole. If he played well, he felt elated and was a jovial companion to the friends who made up his regular foursome. But if he landed in the rough or missed a putt, he became sullen and withdrawn. Moreover, even though he played only social golf, he couldn't tolerate anyone else winning. If another in his foursome was close behind or pulling ahead, Jeff would frequently talk when his friend was swinging. He would also move his own ball to a better position if he thought no one was looking. When his friends suggested that he not take the game so seriously, he looked at them as though they were crazy. He couldn't imagine feeling less intensely because he craved the elation he felt when he won and dreaded the misery he felt when he lost.*

*Eventually, Jeff's friends began to make excuses when he called them to set up a game. Finally, one friend admitted that Jeff's mood swings* and unsportsmanlike behavior were ruining the game for everyone else and that they had found another fourth. It was at this point that Jeff called us.

Jeff knew from the outset that winning meant everything to him, but he was convinced that everyone felt that way. He couldn't imagine any other means to experience that special glow. As the months passed Jeff became increasingly aware that in his head there was always a running stream of negative commentary about himself. For example, when he hit a poor shot, he would call himself "a stupid S.O.B." With that kind of steady self-criticism, it was no wonder that Jeff was driven to experience the pride of winning in order to get temporary relief from his negative feelings about himself.

Once Jeff began to tune into the self-critical thoughts that were always in the background, he was reminded of how inadequate he had felt as a child. His parents and then his teachers had always seemed to expect more of him than he could produce. He told us that, "The only times I can remember feeling that any adult was proud of me was when my team won or I managed to get an 'A.'" Even though he often felt like a failure, Jeff also remembered feeling pleased that his parents and teachers had such high expectations for him.

In the course of treatment, Jeff frequently felt convinced that we were looking down on him for not "getting it" faster or not changing quickly enough. We were able to show him that he was assuming that we would apply the same impossible standards that he had experienced in his childhood and that he now applied to himself.

Jeff began to see that he frequently tried to feel better by treating himself with the same harshness that as a child he had felt he deserved. Jeff took a fresh look at his expectations for himself and realized that they were unreasonable. As a result of all of Jeff's work with us, his self-critical voices began slowly to lose credibility.

As Jeff adopted a more positive and relaxed attitude toward himself, winning no longer seemed the key to his emotional well-being. Little by little he began to enjoy the social aspects of the golf game and to *ride out bad shots and missed putts with more equanimity. He asked his friends to fit him in when they needed a fourth and was relieved and happy to be given a second chance. He found he could now enjoy playing with his friends even when the game didn't go the way he wanted.*

If when you succeed at something you feel a rush of good feelings about yourself you can't get any other way, you are using the pleasure of succeeding to offset feelings of inadequacy and self-doubt. The problem of course is that success doesn't really erase the negative feelings it is meant to soothe and, moreover, success is a shaky foundation on which to rest one's inner well-being. Occasionally, the most talented athlete will lose a game, the smartest student will get a "B," and the most astute businessperson will suffer reverses. Recognizing that you are using success to quiet your self-critical voices and to bolster your self-esteem is the first step toward learning to enjoy a good effort for its own sake regardless of the outcome.

## Seeing Yourself Through the Eyes of Others

Another consequence of depending on externals to feel valuable and worthwhile is that others' opinions of you can take on an exaggerated importance. If you are constantly checking for approval and looking for praise from others, you may find yourself adjusting your appearance, work, or social relating in ways you yourself would not have chosen, and you may find it difficult to know what you really believe or feel. The flip side is that you may be exceedingly sensitive to even a hint of criticism, with the result that constructive suggestions can feel devastating rather than helpful.

### Sandy
*Sandy worked as a clothing designer for a large couture house. She had a wonderful eye for color and a creative and innovative sense of design.*

*But she couldn't feel satisfied with her work unless a friend or coworker liked it as well. She would show a design to others and uncritically implement their suggestions because she valued their opinions more than her own. The result was that her designs were pale shadows of what she could have produced if she were able to believe in her own artistic judgment. Sandy was not getting particularly good job reviews and consulted us with the thought that perhaps she needed a career change.*

*Sandy had grown up in a family that had very high expectations for children. If Sandy drew a picture or wrote a story, her parents and, subsequently, many of her teachers, would suggest that she change it to their liking. In spite of the fact that stories and pictures were artistic creations, Sandy would be told, "Don't make the sun so yellow," or "Why not have a different ending to your story?" When she made the suggested changes, Sandy found that her work received high praise. Because she already felt insecure and inadequate, Sandy needed others' approval to maintain her inner equilibrium. Soon she was painting or writing as a way of getting compliments from others rather than primarily for enjoyment and for herself. She felt so gratified by the praise she received that she never noticed the price she paid, which was to devalue her own creativity.*

*From the beginning Sandy found working with us difficult. Immediately after she shared a thought or experience she wanted to know our opinion. For example, after our first meeting she wanted to know if we thought she should change careers. When we explained that her belief that her opinion didn't count was the problem, and telling her what to do was definitely not the solution, she bitterly accused us of not wanting to help her.*

*Sandy struggled mightily with the pain she felt when we didn't step in and take over her life. Eventually, though, she began to feel cared about in a new and different way. She began to realize that we believed that she was ultimately the most qualified person to make decisions for herself. As her focus shifted from what we thought to what she thought, she experienced the liberation of being the judge of her own creations and actions. Her designs began to reflect this change and her true abilities showed through. Sandy decided for herself that she definitely wanted to continue in the profession she had originally chosen.*

If you are a person who regularly looks to others to evaluate your efforts, you can see that when your parents and important others expected too much of you, you became convinced that your ideas, judgments, and decisions were somehow not good enough and that you felt safer and better when you looked to others for direction. Although their expectations of you were unrealistic, your parents and other adults were trying to help, and did not intend to turn you into an adult who has difficulty believing in yourself. This knowledge will help you recover when the addiction to unhappiness causes you to try to feel better by devaluing your own abilities or by overvaluing others' competence.

## Seeking Comfort Through Unhappiness

If your parents misunderstood your needs or for some reason were unable to attend to them, out of love for your parents and in an attempt to care for yourself exactly as they cared for you, you unknowingly developed the desire to make yourself happy by causing yourself the familiar discomfort you regularly experienced with your parents. The momentous consequence is that while you often make choices that bring you genuine happiness, at other times you may believe you are seeking happiness when in fact you strive to re-create what an outsider would recognize as unhappy feelings.

If without realizing it you developed an appetite for the false pleasure produced by making yourself unhappy, real pleasure can feel unsatisfying. At the same time, you also retain inborn wishes to experience genuine happiness (which is why you can make positive changes in your life by reading these pages). The result is that your life may sometimes feel like an emotional roller coaster.

To varying degrees, each time you experience real happiness, deep down you may feel the absence of the unhappiness you have confused with happiness, and you may try to supply it. We call the reaction to genuine pleasure that causes people unknowingly to seek unhappiness an *aversive reaction to pleasure*. Aversive reactions to pleasure are an expression of the addiction to unhappiness. They explain what in some ways is the most puzzling human behavior—people who "have it all" and then destroy everything.

Aversive reactions to pleasure occur on a daily basis in commonplace ways. A teen we know was invited to the prom by a boy she really liked. Immediately afterward she began to focus on the fact that she had not been invited to a party that some of her friends were attending. Within a short time her good feelings had evaporated and she was feeling miserable and unwanted.

Aversive reactions to pleasure are the reason that people frequently respond to success with depression or actions that are unintentionally self-defeating. You may be able to think of instances in which you achieved success or experienced some other kind of pleasure and then reacted by creating a negative experience for yourself. Perhaps you felt depressed, picked a fight with someone close to you, had an "accident," lost something of value, or forgot to turn in an assignment. At the time, these unpleasant consequences probably seemed unfathomable and "out of the blue." Now you can see that at times when you are experiencing "too much" pleasure, your need for a state of mind that feels familiar or comforting but that is really unhappiness can induce you to re-create the inner discomfort you learned to need as a child.

The good news is that when you can recognize and anticipate aversive reactions to pleasure, you have begun to free yourself from the grip of the heretofore unrecognized addiction to unhappiness.

## Self-Sabotage in Love, Work, and Health

You may have noticed that when you set a goal for yourself, you sometimes have great difficulty keeping your resolve firm until you reach it. Perhaps you put off starting, or you begin full throttle and then run out of gas. Then a friend or neighbor tells you of a new system that "really works" and you try that. The new approach may succeed for a while, but eventually you find that you seem to have lost the will to continue. What you could not have known until now is that most likely an addiction to unhappiness was sabotaging your best efforts. If you had had that knowledge, you might not have been so discouraged when you lost steam or backslid, with the result that it would have been much easier to pick up where you left off and to go on to achieve your goal.

### Elaine

*Elaine was a single woman in her twenties who made a good living as a real estate broker. The problem was that her finances were such a mess that the only way she had any idea of how much money was in her checking account was when her checks started bouncing. Even though Elaine knew that credit card interest was terribly steep, her credit cards were always at their limit. She lost some bills and never got around to paying others, which ruined her credit rating and forced her to pay a higher rate for all types of credit.*

*Elaine herself traced her problem with money to her childhood. Her parents had been comfortable financially but were worried about spoiling Elaine by buying her too much. They put her on a strict allowance and forced her to save for everything she got. Elaine would have to wait for what seemed an eternity to buy a toy she wanted. Keeping track of her money took on the meaning to her of having to face the reality of never having what she wanted or needed.*

*While Elaine's memories focused mainly on times when her parents withheld toys she wanted, it seemed to us that her parents' concerns about spoiling Elaine may also have caused them to withhold the com-*

fort and affection she needed as a much younger child. The addiction to unhappiness she had learned by copying her parents' treatment of her in her early years had eventually crystallized into her conflict about buying things for herself.

Not surprisingly, the moment Elaine was able to take out her own credit cards, she found herself in a struggle to manage her finances. When things got really bad, she consulted financial planners and read popular books about managing her money. She even took a loan to pay off all her credit cards, which she then cut up. But none of these efforts worked because after a time her addiction to unhappiness weakened her resolve. She would fill out and send in one of the new credit card applications that appeared in the mail, lose track of her checks, and buy things she wanted without having any idea whether she could pay for them. Finally, when Elaine's creditors threatened to force her into bankruptcy, she consulted us.

We helped Elaine to see that her problem was not just her disorganized approach to money, but the addiction to unhappiness. She deprived herself to re-create the feelings that as a child she had believed her parents wanted for her. Although on the surface her problem was difficulty managing her finances, the consequence was that she always had to worry about whether or not she could have what she wanted.

There had been nothing wrong with the basic financial reforms that Elaine had tried. The real problem was that she assumed they would work and was completely taken by surprise when her resolve evaporated. Once she became aware of the strength of her need to sabotage her efforts to gain control over her finances, she focused on the problem of keeping her resolve to change. She cut up her credit cards again and discarded unopened letters soliciting her to apply for new ones. She got a checkbook that provided carbons of her checks and used one session with us a month to balance her checkbook against her bank statement. When she began to chafe at using her time with us that way, she chose to balance her checkbook before she came in for her session and then to show us the reconciled account.

*Of course there were still times when Elaine's addiction to making herself unhappy in this way got the upper hand and she would over-spend. But rather than use that slip as an occasion to give up the entire enterprise of getting on top of her financial affairs, she would plan with us to eliminate other expenses in order to make up for the splurge. Gradually, Elaine pulled herself out of debt. For the first time she was able to buy what she needed and wanted without creating financial chaos that would cause her deprivation in the future.*

If there are areas of your life that you repeatedly vow to improve, but you lose your determination on the way to your goal, chances are that this is where the addiction to unhappiness is expressing itself most strongly. In Section II, we offer you specific guidelines for keeping your resolve in the areas of health and fitness, work, and relationships.

## Holding On to Happiness

The addiction to unhappiness may assert itself most insistently whenever you are feeling particularly happy. Perhaps you have just had a career success, made a new friend or fallen in love, lost those pounds that have been plaguing you, or you or someone you love has had good fortune of some kind. Instead of savoring your happiness, you feel depressed, disappointed in yourself, anxious, or irritable. Or perhaps you do something self-destructive: you leave your credit card in a store, trip on a curb you should have seen but didn't and twist your ankle, take a risk in your car that narrowly misses causing an accident, or bounce a check in a highly embarrassing way. Aversive reactions to pleasure can be as mild as temporarily feeling unattractive. They may be as severe as jeopardizing your job or hurting yourself "accidentally."

Perhaps, like most people, you have never noted the connection between feeling good and then becoming unhappy. You may have concluded that both happiness and unhappiness are unpredictable and outside of your control. This feeling of helplessness over one's inner experience is both uncomfortable and disturbing.

Or maybe you have noticed that the pleasure you feel in life often seems to be cut short by unpleasant thoughts or moods, or by things that "go wrong." You may have decided that happiness is fleeting and that it is folly to expect too much out of life.

In either case, of course, the real problem is that an addiction to unhappiness is causing you to feel uncomfortable with "too much" pleasure and to compensate by creating unhappiness in some area of your life.

## Melanie

*Melanie constantly caused problems for herself whenever things were going well. If she were feeling particularly successful and competent, she would often forget to keep a date she had made and leave a friend sitting alone in a restaurant, or she would lose her wallet, or lock her keys in her car. She had no idea that these incidents represented aversive reactions to feeling happy. Each unpleasant event seemed to come out of left field. Melanie would react by resolving to be more careful. She would be vigilant for a while, but eventually she would inconvenience herself again. When she locked her keys in the car with the motor running and missed a critical meeting at work, she decided to seek help.*

*We encouraged Melanie to reflect on what had been happening in her life just before she had locked the keys in the car. She realized that she had been feeling particularly happy because she had just gotten a promotion. As she worked with us, Melanie realized that whenever she felt happy she would feel a subtle anxiety that was not eased until the happy feelings were gone. Locking her keys in her car was just one manifestation of her unrecognized need to regain her inner equilibrium by causing herself discomfort.*

*Melanie also had a chance to see how her aversive reactions to pleasure manifested themselves in her relationship with us. On more than one occasion when she had particularly enjoyed her session and eagerly anticipated seeing us again, she forgot to set her alarm and slept through the next appointment. Once she forgot to take the correct exit* off the highway and made herself 20 minutes late. More than any other experience, times when she inadvertently sabotaged the pleasure she was anticipating with us convinced her that she was struggling with an addiction to unhappiness.

At her request, we helped Melanie develop a plan to combat her aversive reactions to pleasure. Whenever she felt particularly upbeat, she immediately thought to look at her keys as she exited the car. She put in a wake-up call with the telephone company on days when she had an appointment with us. She put Post-it notes on the refrigerator to remind herself of social dates and birthdays.

We cautioned Melanie that her needs to make herself unhappy might temporarily become stronger in response to her new resolve to hang on to happiness. To ward off these reactions she made extra car keys and taped them to the bottom of her car, and she asked her friends to call and remind her shortly before they were to meet. Interestingly, when Melanie succeeded in heading off an aversive reaction, she would often have a nightmare in which she fell into the trap she had avoided during the day. For example, after a friend called as planned and reminded her of a luncheon engagement that Melanie would otherwise have forgotten, Melanie told us, "I dreamed that I left my friend sitting alone in a restaurant while I remained at my desk working." Melanie could see how much progress was represented by the fact that her addiction to unhappiness could only get the upper hand in her dreams.

If you begin to observe the ways in which you make life difficult for yourself just at moments when you are feeling especially happy, you will see that life is not as fickle and unpredictable as it seemed. *You are the author of your own life to an extent you probably never knew.* With this newfound sense of empowerment and the strategies you will find in Section II for overcoming aversive reactions to pleasure, you will be able to find ways to anticipate these reactions and prevent them from happening.

## Undermining Your Victory

You may be one of those people who perseveres until you reach a goal, only to see your hard-won victory slip away. The goal may be as small as taking up jogging or as large as becoming a manager in your company. The reverses that occur may surprise you given the months and even years you may have spent working diligently, and you may find it very difficult to see that these reverses result from your aversive reaction to the good feelings that success brought. The connection may be especially difficult to make if your success is undermined by a problem that appears unrelated, such as drinking too much, engaging in risky behavior, or becoming depressed, or if you remain successful but find yourself unable to enjoy your achievement.

### Seth

*A business executive, Seth rose from poverty to become a pillar of his community. He served on the boards of the local symphony and art museum and on blue-ribbon commissions for governmental reform. Seth adored his wife and was a proud and loving father to his four children. All the while, however, he neglected his own affairs. Most importantly, although he was exceedingly wealthy, he never got around to paying his income taxes. After seven years in which he paid no tax at all, he realized that he had placed himself in terrible jeopardy and came to see us.*

*As we worked together, he recollected that even as a child he had sabotaged his success. For example, his outstanding diving ability had won him a scholarship to an excellent college that his parents could never have afforded. Shortly after he made the varsity team in his second year of college, he began to take chances by diving too close to the board. Finally, he hit his back on the board so hard that he cracked a vertebra and had to retire from diving. Of course, he had not realized at the time that his risk taking and injury were an aversive reaction to the pleasure he felt at receiving a scholarship and succeeding as a collegiate diver. He now saw* that his failure to pay taxes resulted from the same need to poison the fruits of his hard work.

As he understood himself better, Seth determined not to let his addiction to unhappiness ruin his life. He engaged an attorney and successfully avoided prosecution by approaching the internal revenue service with a plan to pay the back taxes plus interest and penalties. He hired an accountant to manage his personal finances, and told her to hound him until he turned in the raw data needed to file his tax return every year. Seth learned to keep an eye out for other ways in which he was tempted to engage in risky behavior. For example, he realized that when he was by himself he often drove too fast for the road conditions.

Over time, Seth grew able to enjoy his life without causing himself reactive suffering. His aversive reactions were reduced to minor annoyances, such as leaving a book he was reading on a plane. Seth realized that these minor setbacks were in reaction to the tremendous progress he was making. He used them as occasions to renew his resolve to enjoy the life he had worked so hard to create for himself.

There are people who undermine their success in ways that are invisible to them because the discomfort they cause themselves fits with values they learned in childhood and feels deserved.

### Sophie

Sophie worked for years building a successful public relations firm. She was written up in magazines and asked to speak at national conferences. Yet her business was in danger of going under because she had begun to find it exceedingly difficult either to bill her clients or to collect from those she had billed. She felt uncomfortable at the thought of "chasing" after the money that was owed her and said that the money was "not really the point." Fortunately, she listened to her friends' concerns about the way she was jeopardizing her business and consulted us.

As far back as she could remember, Sophie had had deep feelings of being undeserving. Being selfless, that is, putting herself last, made her feel worthwhile and happy. As long as she was working for someone else, she consistently performed at a high level, although she always found it difficult to take credit for her good ideas. When the company she worked for was acquired by a larger company, she started her own firm.

While the business was in the process of getting off the ground, Sophie did a fairly effective job of billing. When her firm got good notices and became successful, however, Sophie experienced increasing difficulty billing and collecting. Sophie could say only that she felt distaste for the entire billing process. The more successful she became, the stronger became her conscious need to feel virtuous by not collecting what was due her.

We explained to Sophie that her inner equilibrium was maintained by two incompatible sources of well-being: the genuine pleasure of valuing and taking good care of herself, and the false pleasure (unhappiness in disguise) of feeling undeserving. Her success had disrupted this balance and she was trying to restore her equilibrium by sabotaging her hard-won achievement. Her addiction to feeling worthwhile by experiencing the pain of feeling undeserving was effectively concealed behind the pleasure she felt at giving up the money that was due her.

For a while Sophie was unable to understand what we were saying because she felt so virtuous when she refused to focus on billing or collecting what was owed. Not surprisingly, whenever we gave her a bill, she angrily concluded that we were concerned about money and not about her. She said that if we really cared about her we wouldn't need to be paid. It seemed impossible to her that we could both genuinely want to help and also feel that we deserved compensation for our professional efforts.

As months passed and Sophie's work with us progressed, she admitted to herself that we did seem committed to her welfare even though we also *continued to bill her. Yet she was unable to apply the same reasoning to her own efforts on behalf of her clients. Eventually, though, she saw that she helped her clients by doing good work for them, not by undervaluing her own efforts. It was not long before she realized that the act of depriving herself, which had made her happy because it seemed selfless, was not a social virtue, but rather was an expression of the addiction to unhappiness.*

*While Sophie now wished to change, she doubted that she had the inner strength to put this resolution into practice by herself. At our suggestion she hired a part-time bookkeeper whose only function was billing and collections. When she was tempted to instruct the bookkeeper not to bill a client or to overlook a debt, she spoke with us first, and usually managed to refrain from interfering. Sophie discovered firsthand that she was happiest feeling that her work was valuable and deserved to be compensated.*

If you find that you reach a goal you care about and have worked hard to attain only to undermine it in some way, you are seeing the effects of the addiction to unhappiness. In Section II we will help you learn to preserve and enhance the successes you have attained.

## Addictions to Eating, Drinking, Sex, and Work

Most addictions are an expression of the addiction to unhappiness, and can be understood as a type of aversive reaction to pleasure. Addictions have remained both mysterious and difficult to remedy. Recently there have been efforts to explain them as the result of genetically determined chemical imbalances or brain structure, but these efforts have not yielded conclusive evidence. The strongest evidence shows that addictions are not "hardwired" into our brains but result from learned needs for unhappiness. It is just because addictions are learned behaviors that many addicted individuals are able to turn away from their addictive behavior with the help of a psychotherapeutic process or by participation in relationship-oriented peer groups.

Most addicted behavior is an expression of the conflicting desires that cause aversive reactions to pleasure. We have just discussed the type of aversive reaction to pleasure in which an individual swings back and forth between happiness and unhappiness. Experiences of genuine pleasure are followed by the unrecognized need to experience unhappiness, while experiences of unhappiness result in a striving for constructive pleasure.

In contrast, the inner well-being of many addicted individuals is sustained by the *simultaneous* gratification of these two incompatible motives. In other words, addicted individuals can unknowingly fuse two fundamentally incompatible sources of inner well-being—genuine pleasure and destructive pleasure (pleasure that really serves to gratify the addiction to unhappiness). The overeater taints the genuine pleasure of eating with the misery caused by overeating. In the majority of addictions, individuals pursue an inherently pleasurable experience to such an extreme that it causes unhappiness. In addition to those who overeat, some people overwork, overexercise, are constantly in search of new sexual conquests, or drink too much.

### Eleanor

*Eleanor came from a family in which food rather than physical affection was an important symbol of love. As an infant and small child, Eleanor was rarely cuddled and she learned to accept the lack of closeness and to turn to her own thumb for comfort. As she grew older and came home from school upset about a test that didn't go well or a fight with a friend, she would feel virtuous when she resisted the temptation to "bother" her parents with her troubles. Instead of going to them for sympathy and a hug, she would retreat to her room and find solace in a candy bar.*

*By the time she reached adolescence, Eleanor regularly turned to food for soothing, especially when things went wrong. She gained weight, stopped exercising when she felt too embarrassed to be seen in athletic clothes, and then became seriously overweight. She tried diet after diet without success. In her twenties she was diagnosed with high* blood pressure and told she must lose weight. Still unable to control her eating, she consulted us.

Eleanor came in feeling like a complete failure. She felt that she lacked the motivation and will power that kept her friends at a normal weight. As we worked with her, she began to realize that without knowing it, she had grown up believing that the physical isolation and loneliness she experienced as a young child represented love and happiness her parents meant for her. When she combined the need to feel good by re-creating these (unhappy) feelings with the use of food to replace love and affection, the result was a drive to use eating to make herself simultaneously miserable and soothed.

We helped Eleanor to think about the pleasure of eating as separate from the misery of overeating. As she realized that she was using food as a source of suffering as well as of enjoyment, Eleanor found a new source of pleasure in listening carefully to her own body. Rather than focusing on what she wanted to eat, she began to think about whether or not she was hungry. If she wasn't hungry, she tried to find other sources of satisfaction. At first she chose sedentary activities like reading a book or watching TV, but as the weight began to come off, Eleanor found that she loved bike riding. She joined a bike club, which made the process of losing weight more enjoyable.

Eleanor knew from working with us that as her preference for genuine pleasure grew stronger, her needs to feel the kind of well-being that came from seeking a destructive type of pleasure would rebound. She was prepared for the incidents of overeating that had previously caused her to abandon a diet. When she gorged herself, she was able for the first time to resist the voice that said, "See, you might as well give up, you can't do it—you've undone all your hard work." With our encouragement, each time she binged she rededicated herself to her diet. As time went on, Eleanor learned how to anticipate moments of backsliding and to minimize them. When she felt the need to overeat grow stronger, she made quantities of popcorn or other foods that would satisfy her need to overeat in ways that were less damaging to *her efforts to lose weight. Over a two-year period, Eleanor was able to lose and then to keep off the pounds necessary to get her blood pressure down and to feel normal and healthy.*

The balance between genuine and destructive pleasure can vary. For example, people who are addicted to gambling or illegal substances experience little constructive pleasure and much destructive pleasure.

Once addicted people realize that they are in the grip of the need for destructive as well as constructive pleasure, and that from an early age their primary happiness has been composed of these two diametrically opposed sources of well-being, they can begin the process of choosing pleasures unaccompanied by negative side effects.

# Section 2

# Choosing Happiness

In Chapters 4 through 7, we show you how to use what you learned in Section I to take charge of and transform your life. Our most important message is that *you are never too old and it is never too late to recover from an addiction to unhappiness and embark on a life of positive, satisfying, and effective choices.* The spark of inborn joy and optimism that you possessed when you entered the world is never extinguished by the presence of an addiction to unhappiness. It can be fanned into a guiding flame by thoughtful, careful life planning.

If you have an addiction to unhappiness, you will find that facing it is both liberating and empowering. Like many people, you may have concluded that important parts of your life are out of your control. Certainly, we are all to varying degrees affected by chance, but *chance does not have to determine the true quality of our lives.* Even when you are faced with the most unfortunate of events, you can learn to maintain your inner equilibrium and to avoid seeking comfort by turning on yourself or others.

In other words, you may not recognize it, but you are the author of the meaningful aspects of your life, both pleasant and unpleasant. This knowledge is the key to gaining control over the addiction to unhappiness and to making every part of your life rewarding and enjoyable.

If you have been suffering from the addiction to unhappiness and its workings have been mostly invisible to you, you have probably not had a real choice about the way in which you live your life. Even with the sincerest intention to make good choices for yourself, you may unknowingly have undermined many of your best efforts. Once the struggle between the learned though unrecognized need to make yourself unhappy and your inborn capacity for genuine happiness is out in the open, you will find it much easier to turn away from the unhappiness that has always felt familiar and inevitable. You will be able to opt for satisfying relationships, success at work, a healthy lifestyle, emotional stability, and a generally good life.

Equally important, knowing about the addiction to unhappiness will prepare you for the moments of backsliding that can follow your efforts to change. We define backsliding as *difficulty following through on a resolution*. When you know that positive choices can unbalance your inner equilibrium, you will not be surprised or discouraged to find yourself losing your resolve and even slipping back toward the place from which you started. You can learn to experience these times of backsliding as part of the healing process rather than as a failure of will.

You have probably always thought of yourself as a unitary being. We are suggesting that you begin to think of yourself as owning competing and incompatible motives: (1) for genuine pleasure and (2) for the unhappiness (false pleasure) you long ago confused with genuine pleasure. The momentous consequence of this realization is that you must evaluate the quality of your decisions. *The fact that a particular choice appeals to you is no guarantee that it will bring you genuine pleasure.* For example, the driver who decides to press ahead and stay on schedule even though he is feeling sleepy may feel that he is making the right decision. But in reality the addiction to unhappiness is causing him to choose the false pleasure of staying on schedule under risky conditions over the genuine pleasure of putting safety first.

One of the most important lessons you will learn here is that you always need to ask yourself whether the choice you are contemplating feels attractive because it satisfies the addiction to unhappiness or because it satisfies your inborn desire for genuine pleasure. An example is the dieter who feels irresistibly drawn to the candy bars at the supermarket checkout. The realization that the anticipated pleasure of eating the candy bar will actually gratify the addiction to unhappiness by undermining the genuine pleasure of reaching a healthy weight will make it much easier to resist.

## The Road Back: Phases of Recovery

The phases in overcoming the addiction to unhappiness are:

- Getting started (even when you don't feel like it)
- Coping with episodes of backsliding
- Keeping your resolve when it starts to evaporate
- Thinking of yourself as a recovering addict to unhappiness

Each phase requires different kinds of planning and vigilance. You will learn that *the true definition of progress is "more successes than failures over time,"* so that you can react positively to relapses. In the pages that follow we give you a general description of the phases of what we call the *Lifeplan*. Then, in Chapters 4 through 7, we show you how to navigate these phases successfully to improve your emotional life, health, relationships, and work experience.

## Getting Started (Even When You Don't Feel Like It)

No matter which aspects of your life you want to improve, getting started can be a significant hurdle. Most people know exactly what they *should* do (they need to lose weight, eat better, exercise, get their work done, stop smoking, balance their checkbooks, spend enjoyable time with their loved ones, etc.) but they often find it difficult to act on their decision to change. They postpone the start date—until after the New Year, after they finish a big project at work, after a trip, after a birthday, or just anytime other than now.

The problem, of course, is that merely setting the time when you will change your life for the better feels like progress, so it is easy to mistake the resolution for the deed. As long as the day when you will implement your good intentions lies in the future, you don't have to struggle with the addiction to unhappiness. As the day approaches, however, your resolve begins to waver. You become aware that changing your life for the better is going to involve an unpleasant internal battle, and you may react by postponing the start date. That returns you to the pleasant feeling that you are moving forward and avoids the internal confrontation that would be engaged the moment you take the first step. And, of course, when you don't begin, you restore the familiar state of discomfort you have been living with for so long, thereby gratifying the addiction to unhappiness.

If you are a person who knows what improvements you want to make in your life, but you can't get started because you keep postponing the first step, most likely you are being intimidated by the internal conflict you feel brewing as the start date nears. The threat of inner resistance may cause you to delay starting in hopes that after a specified time (the New Year, your vacation) it will be easier to begin. In truth, when the problem is the addiction to unhappiness and not your timing, the first step will never feel easy. Making constructive choices for yourself may always be challenging because you are giving up some of the unhappiness you have confused with happiness. If you wait to begin until you "feel like it," you will postpone the rest of your life.

The following strategies will help you take the first step toward the improvements you want to make:

- *Start with a small project.* Identify a fairly modest goal (for example, to walk a half mile a day for 10 days, to lose three pounds, to balance your checkbook for three months, to spend an hour of enjoyable time with a friend or partner, to start on a report the day you get it, etc.). Many people take on nearly impossible goals (to lose five pounds a week, to run a marathon after two months, to save money by never, ever eating out). They fail immediately and then give up.

- *Set a start date that is no more than a few days off.*
- *Decide that no matter how appealing calls for delay sound, you will ignore them and go ahead with your plan.* Prepare yourself for the fact that as the day nears, you may begin to feel that you really don't want to do this anymore, that you are too busy to get started, or that it would be much easier to accomplish this next week or next month. If your best intentions aren't strong enough and you give in to the temptation to postpone, renew your determination to conquer the internal forces that want you to be unhappy and set a new date in the near future.
- *When the day comes, take your first step, knowing that it may feel hard because your resolve may have weakened.*
- *Do something genuinely nice for yourself to mark the fact that you got started.*

Taking the first step toward your goal is a meaningful accomplishment. Immediately, though, you need to prepare for the next phase in your struggle for happiness.

## Backsliding Is Part of the Healing Process

Most programs designed to help you improve your life make the misleading assumption that you will easily follow the steps they outline. You yourself may believe that once you identify a self-improvement goal and take the first step toward it, it is only a question of putting one foot in front of the other. So when the first experience of backsliding occurs (you sleep in and don't exercise, you eat a big piece of the chocolate cake your host baked, you watch TV instead of starting a report, you forget to enter some expenditures and bounce a check), you may feel startled and discouraged. When the next setback occurs, you may conclude that you chose a goal that was too ambitious and you give up altogether.

Recognition of the following precept will make it more difficult for setbacks to derail your resolution to improve your life: *Because of the addiction to unhappiness, backsliding is not only inevitable, it is a part of the healing process.* You genuinely desire to change your life for the better and to realize your birthright of genuine happiness. At the same time, a significant portion of your good feelings about yourself come from causing yourself the familiar unhappiness you long ago confused with happiness. When you embark on a program of positive improvement, you immediately feel the absence of that familiar, comfortable unhappiness and you try to supply it by sabotaging your efforts. In other words, backsliding is a type of aversive reaction to pleasure (see Section I). You can see that it is also an inevitable part of the healing process.

Once you know that at every moment you need to supply yourself with two incompatible sources of inner well-being—genuine happiness and false happiness, which is really unhappiness in disguise—you can see that the process of improving your life will never proceed in a straight line. Real progress is better described using the metaphor of a tennis match. When you lose a point in a tennis game, you don't give up because you know that you can still win the match. Similarly, you can think of backsliding as nothing more than a point won by the addiction to unhappiness. As long as over time you win more than you lose, you will be victorious.

There is an enormous difference between feeling ambushed and defeated by moments of backsliding and viewing them as an integral part of the healing process. When you recognize that setbacks are natural and expectable, it is much easier to keep your eye on your goal, pick yourself up, and renew your determination.

Moreover, when you know to expect setbacks and are not thrown by them, you will find that you can use them to your advantage to make yourself less vulnerable to backsliding in the future. If you are trying to lose weight and in spite of your best intentions you stop at the bakery on the way home and blow your diet, rather than concluding that you lack the willpower to lose weight, you can decide that from then on you will take a different route home.

Episodes of backsliding can occur at any point on the way to your chosen goal, but usually after you have weathered a number of these setbacks and know that you can get through and beyond them, you will be less daunted by them. Keeping your resolve is another matter entirely. Paradoxically, the more progress you make, the more your resolve is likely to waver.

## *Keeping Your Resolve When It Starts to Evaporate*

As you approach your goal, chances are that you will find your resolve weakening. This loss of willpower can take many forms. Some of the most common are:

- You lose touch with your reason for changing and can't imagine why you ever embarked on a course that makes life feel so difficult. After a prolonged internal struggle, a man we know finally managed to break up with a woman who constantly deprecated him. Two months later, he remembered only her good qualities, missed her terribly, and couldn't think of why he had left her. He called her and resumed the relationship.
- You conclude that even though it is short of your goal, the place you have reached is "good enough." You decide that you don't need to lose all 10 pounds, because you look better, now that you have lost 5 pounds.

- You feel bored with the efforts you are making. You begin to feel that exercising is deadly dull and can't get yourself out the door.
- You feel exhausted from having to fight so hard to make things different and consequently give up the battle. A woman we know finally got her checkbook balanced for the first time in years. As the months passed, it felt harder and harder to force herself to sit down and reconcile her bank statement. She decided she couldn't face the struggle she went through every time she sat down to look at her finances. When the next bank statement arrived, she shoved it in a drawer.

The reason for losing steam after making progress toward a goal you had set is that most likely your resolve was undermined by the addiction to unhappiness. The more you taste genuine happiness, the stronger becomes your reactive need for the old, familiar nourishment of unhappiness masquerading as happiness. This is the explanation for the common phenomenon that the closer you get to a positive goal, the less valuable it seems. With this understanding, and with the specific strategies we will give you in the next four chapters, you will be able to renew your resolve when it starts to flag and to push ahead and finish making the improvements you have worked so hard to bring about.

## Thinking of Yourself as a Recovering Addict to Unhappiness

If you follow the guidelines and strategies for navigating the first three phases in overcoming the addiction to unhappiness set forth here and in the next four chapters, you will eventually reach the personal goals you set. At that point it may be tempting to bask in the pleasure your hard work has brought you and to lower your guard. If you have achieved a goal in the past only to find that when you weren't looking your success evaporated or was undermined, you know firsthand that vigilance is still necessary.

It is true that success breeds success. You will find that the more you are able to use what you learn here to neutralize the addiction to unhappiness and to move ahead with the choices you want to make, the happier and more empowered you will feel. The false pleasure produced by the familiar types of unhappiness you have always found soothing pales when it is contrasted with the genuine pleasure of making positive, self-caring choices. For example, once you begin to experience the true pleasure of responding compassionately and constructively rather than angrily or self-critically when things go wrong, the false pleasure of anger and self-criticism loses much of its former appeal.

Still, because until now you have spent your life believing that you wanted nothing but happiness for yourself when at least part of the time you were unknowingly seeking unhappiness, your need for those familiar feelings of unhappiness lingers on for a long while. This is why you can't rest on your laurels and why it is helpful to think of yourself as a recovering addict to unhappiness.

When you make it up the mountain and are enjoying the view from the top, keep an eye out for your need to unseat yourself. The addiction to unhappiness can undermine your success in many different ways. The most common is that you give up some of the gains you have made—you put some or all of the pounds back on, you stop exercising, you procrastinate and stop meeting deadlines. But you may also find that you are causing yourself problems in areas that seem unrelated to your success—you hurt yourself "accidentally," you pick a fight with a loved one, you feel anxious or down. The unhappiness that results can either taint the pleasure you have been feeling or make it difficult for you to maintain your gains.

Once you reach a sought-for personal goal, you need to keep a keen eye out to ensure both that you maintain the ground you have gained, and also that you don't reactively cause yourself problems in some other area of your life. If you slip, the prescription is the same as before—realize that some backsliding is inevitable, that it in no way detracts from the success you have achieved, and rededicate yourself to your goal.

Over time, as you increasingly experience the genuine pleasure of choosing the life you want and you also become accomplished at keeping the addiction to unhappiness at bay, the long-standing appeal of unhappiness will fade. You will have found for yourself the real happiness you were born to know. With minimal vigilance you will then be able to make positive choices in every area of your life and to avoid turning on yourself or others when things do not go as planned or hoped.

# Chapter 4

# Freeing Yourself from Painful Moods

If you are a person who regularly suffers from unfounded fears, anger, or suspicions, guilt, anxiety, depression, mood swings, or phobias, you probably have a deeply held and understandable conviction that you have no control over these emotions. Without a doubt, there is a sense in which this belief is accurate. If you are walking and experience a leg cramp, you can stop and rest until it feels better, but if you are feeling emotional pain, there is no obvious remedy.

We will show you how to become much more in charge of your emotions. Painful emotions that occur without an obvious cause or persist long after the upsetting event that triggered them are one expression of the addiction to unhappiness. Without realizing it, people may seek out painful emotions because early in their lives they misidentified them as the way they were supposed to feel. They unknowingly confused painful emotions with happiness and, as a result, developed a need to reexperience them. It is in this sense that emotional pain is purposeful, even though it is certainly not on purpose.

While it may be surprising and somewhat disconcerting to find that in an important sense you are the author of your emotions, this knowledge also empowers you. Because painful moods are habits learned in childhood, not inborn traits, they can be unlearned. Once that happens, you will be free from self-caused unhappiness. You will consistently be able to choose positive moods and emotions, which will be affected only by truly upsetting life events.

Part of the unlearning process is gaining the ability to distinguish "appropriate" unhappiness from "gratuitous" unhappiness. *Appropriate* unhappiness is a realistic response to an upsetting event. *Gratuitous* unhappiness is an overreaction or sought-for experience that is used to satisfy the addiction to unhappiness. Sadness in response to a significant loss is inevitable. If gratuitous unhappiness is present, the response may also include depression or anxiety that is out of proportion to the actual loss or lasts for months or years. The response makes it difficult to function, causes unfounded anger at or suspicion of others, or promotes a conviction of being unworthy or blameworthy. For example, a man we know experienced gratuitous unhappiness when his car broke down on a vacation, necessitating that he and his family wait a day or two before continuing their trip. His wife and children invited him to join them for family fun in the motel pool. But the anxiety he felt at the breakdown and the resulting delay was so painful that he could get relief only by remaining in the garage and monitoring the progress the mechanic was making on his car. The overwhelming anxiety caused by the addiction to unhappiness kept him from making the best of the situation and enjoying some leisure time with his family.

Gratuitous unhappiness can also occur when a person unknowingly seeks to experience painful emotions as a way of gratifying the addiction to unhappiness. An example is the woman who worked diligently for three years on a novel only to become very depressed in reaction to having it accepted by a publisher.

In this chapter, we will show you how to anticipate and then to begin to liberate yourself from gratuitous emotional suffering. As with all efforts you make to improve your life, backsliding is part of the healing process and not a sign that the way is too hard or the goal unattainable.

## Debunking Myths About Personality

Perhaps the most common misconceptions about personality are that (1) it is set at birth and (2) there is something about people's brain chemistry that "makes them that way." These erroneous beliefs have been very durable, in spite of the fact that there is no convincing evidence that inborn traits or brain chemistry are determining causes of personality. It is true that there is a physical basis for our minds, namely, a functioning brain. However, *the personal, meaningful aspects of our inner life are determined by the quality of the emotions we learned to think of as happiness when we were children and that we seek out today as adults.*

It may be superficially comforting to think that painful emotional states are due to something amiss in our brain structure and, consequently, that we play no role in determining our moods. But at the same time, this notion is profoundly discouraging because it puts the process of regulating our emotions permanently beyond our voluntary control. The reality that we are the actual, though unknowing, authors of our most important emotions is a positive finding because it preserves the possibility that we can choose to improve the quality of our inner lives.

Many people find it difficult to believe that unpleasant emotions that arise seemingly out of nowhere are both acquired and purposeful. They are convinced that an angry, depressed, or anxious person was "that way" from birth onwards or developed these painful moods as a direct result of unfolding biological forces. It is true that some babies are unusually irritable at birth even though they have no physical problems that are causing them pain. But every baby has had nine months of prenatal experiences that to some degree shape the baby's emotional responses. Research has shown that fetuses of mothers who are very stressed or depressed produce unusually high levels of stress hormones in response to stimulation, and that these stress hormones remain elevated much longer than do those of other fetuses. It is not surprising that at birth these babies are more irritable than other babies.

However, with informed parenting, babies who are abnormally irritable at birth do develop into calm, resilient children. This would not be the case if irritability were "hardwired" into their brains.

Some readers may be wondering: "But we know that medications that affect brain chemistry help people with painful emotions like depression or anxiety. Isn't that proof that these painful moods are biochemical in origin?" The fact that some medications can improve an individual's emotional well-being is not evidence that the cause of the individual's emotional distress was biochemical. For one thing, medications are likely to have a "placebo effect." That is, just the fact that someone in authority is making an intervention that promises help can cause people to feel better. There are respectable studies that show that many of the most popular psychological medications are actually no more effective than sugar pills if the people taking them do not know which pill they are taking.

Moreover, when medications succeed in dulling a person's emotional pain, this effect in no way speaks to the *cause* of the individual's emotional pain. If a chemical makes your emotional pain less acute, this does not mean that the source of your bad feelings is a chemical imbalance. To illustrate, if you have a headache and take an analgesic that makes the headache disappear, you still have no idea whether the headache was triggered by emotional upset, fumes, a vascular problem, or some other cause. Suppressing emotional pain is not the same as understanding it and curing it. Furthermore, all brain-altering medications have side effects, which range from serious physical consequences to the subjective experience of being "less awake" in other ways.

Perhaps the strongest evidence in support of the assertion that the primary cause of emotional pain is not biochemical is clinical evidence confirming that competent psychological help can release people from the emotional roller coaster that has made their lives so unpleasant. If painful emotions were truly hardwired, the talking cure of psychotherapy would not work.

Many investigators, ourselves included, have shown that even the most intractable emotional problems can be remedied by psychotherapeutic intervention. At one time we ran a demonstration program designed to help so-called untreatable adolescents. The Illinois Department of Mental Health selected the most violent and treatment-resistant teens in their system. These adolescents were so dangerous that no treatment program in the country could keep them or would take them. When we met them they were facing a lifetime in high-security holding institutions. These adolescents could react to the slightest disappointment or, even to a positive moment, by becoming homicidally angry. Because their early years had been filled with physical and emotional abuse, the particular form of unhappiness they had confused with happiness was saturated with violence and was extremely destructive to themselves and others.

To illustrate, one of the teens confided to his therapist that the reason he was afraid to go to school was that he had been fooling everyone by pretending to read when, in fact, he could hardly read at all. Shortly after, he ran outside and threw a rock through his therapist's car window. The genuine pleasure of sharing a "shameful" secret with an understanding adult deprived him of the unhappiness of feeling alienated from everyone, which he had long ago confused with happiness and found comforting. Without realizing it, he tried to recapture that false pleasure (unhappiness in disguise) by feeling furious with his therapist and damaging his car. The therapist told the boy that he knew how upset he had been feeling but that he couldn't express his anger in that form, and he privately resolved never to leave his car in plain view. At the same time, he helped the teen to see that his behavior was a reaction to the progress he had made in letting himself feel close to the therapist by sharing an intimate secret.

When we offered the adolescents psychological treatment designed to overcome their addiction to unhappiness, all of them improved dramatically. Even though a change in state administrations caused the funding for our program to be terminated prematurely, the adolescents were all sufficiently improved to be mainstreamed back into their communities. To our knowledge, with one exception (which we predicted would occur as a result of the premature termination of the program), they remain functional members of society. (This project is described in greater detail in Katherine Tyson, *New Foundations for Scientific, Social, and Behavioral Research: The Heuristic Paradigm*, Allyn and Bacon, Boston, 1995.)

## Painful Moods Are a Form of Comfort Learned in Childhood

As we described in Section I, every person is born feeling loveable, loved, and loving. When children's emotional needs are satisfied, their inner well-being stabilizes. As adults, these individuals will retain their conviction of being loveable and loving even when they encounter ill fortune. Equally important, they will never cause themselves or others any type of gratuitous unhappiness.

When children's emotional needs are not adequately met, they unknowingly assume that the unhappiness they feel is desirable because it is what their perfect parents want for them. Once they have confused unhappiness with happiness, they develop needs to reexperience these unhappy feelings. They unknowingly begin to seek unhappiness under the misapprehension that it is good and good for them. The unhappiness to which people become addicted can lead them to hurt themselves, to have trouble finding and maintaining close relationships, and to have difficulty working to their potential.

The unhappiness to which people can become addicted may take the form of painful feelings. This makes sense, because when children's emotional needs are not met, they may feel ashamed, depressed, anxious, frightened, or angry. Without knowing it, they assume that these feelings are good because they are convinced that their parents want them to feel this way. They turn to these feelings for soothing as they are growing and when they are adults.

## Painful Moods Are Purposeful, Though Not on Purpose

If you suffer from anxiety, depression, unfounded guilt, irritability, or other unpleasant emotions, you probably experience these feelings as coming "out of nowhere." However, without realizing it you turn to these emotions because in early childhood you confused them with good feelings your parents wanted for you and you wanted for yourself. Now you turn to them to feel "good," to comfort yourself when you have experienced a loss, or in reaction to having "too much" positive pleasure.

It is in this sense that unpleasant emotions are purposeful, even though they feel externally imposed. The benefit of discovering that you are the author of your emotions is that you will find that you have the power to choose good feelings over bad.

## You Are the Author of Your Dreams

Just as with your emotions, you are the real author of your dreams. When people consider the nature of dreams, they tend to forget that dreams are as much the product of the mind as are daydreams or logical analyses. *Even when they are unpleasant or frightening, our dreams provide us with experiences we seek, both knowingly and unknowingly.*

Dreams can satisfy both needs for genuine happiness and also acquired needs for unhappiness. Moreover, the same dream can be used to satisfy both needs.

### Libby
*After many sessions with us and much hard work, Libby was getting ready to leave an abusive relationship. The day after she rented a new apartment in preparation for moving out, she dreamed that she moved into the new apartment only to discover that the partner she was leaving was already living there. She knew from her work with us that the reason she dreamed that her partner had followed her and moved in with her was that her addiction to unhappiness was*

causing her to create in her dreams the false pleasure of the abusive relationship she was giving up.

Libby's parents had been very strict disciplinarians and had sent her to schools that also punished students harshly for misdemeanors. She had understandably misidentified the harsh treatment she received as a way of being loved. Without realizing it, she had continued to pursue this kind of "affection." Libby knew that it was a sign of progress that she was confining her need to feel cared for by creating abusive situations to her dreams, while at the same time she was taking the steps that would end this unhappiness in real life.

It is often the case that when you begin to make progress toward your goal, you find yourself having nightmares. The more progress you make, the more nightmares you may have. These nightmares are a form of anger at yourself for allowing yourself the genuine pleasure of moving toward your goal, which means depriving yourself of the familiar unhappiness you have unknowingly confused with happiness.

### David

David, a plant manager, was seeing us because he was in danger of being fired for being too harsh to those working under him. After a day in which he managed to keep his temper when a worker made a mistake that stopped the production line, he dreamed that he was doing paper work at his desk when his boss appeared and fired him on the spot. Then all of his workers taunted him, threatened him with their tools, and chased him out of the plant.

He was very shaken by this nightmare until he understood that it represented the anger he felt at himself for making things better for himself by controlling his temper at work. The nightmare satisfied his addiction to unhappiness by vividly enacting the self-destructive impulses and resulting emotional pain that he had managed to avert during his waking hours.

## Unlearning Painful Moods

Because the painful emotions that interfere with your ability to live the life you want are the acquired result of your early confusion of unhappiness with happiness, and because they are in continuous competition with your inborn, still-potent desire to experience genuine happiness, they can be unlearned and left behind. In our clinical practices we have repeatedly seen individuals free themselves from the depression, anxiety, unfounded guilt, and other painful feelings that had plagued them for years.

The following is an overview of the guidelines that will help you to recover from gratuitous unhappiness:

- *Accept the fact that there is a way in which, unknown to yourself, feeling badly also makes you feel comfortable or comforted.* There is a wide range of painful emotions that can feel familiar and, therefore, soothing, including: depression, anxiety, fear (phobias), lack of purpose, helplessness, anger, suspicion, loneliness, and self-criticism.
- *Next, try to identify when you are most likely to seek out painful emotions.* Some people are most vulnerable when they are feeling particularly happy. A woman we know reacted to the excitement of falling in love by feeling constant terror that her boyfriend, who traveled frequently on business, would die in a plane crash. Other individuals sometimes fall into painful emotional states as a way of soothing themselves when something goes wrong in their lives. An account executive who lost a large client was so overcome by self-blame that he was unable to take the steps necessary to replace the client.
- *Once you know under what circumstances you are likely to slip into a painful mood, you may find that anticipating it will enable you to head it off.* If not, at least you will have the painful emotion in better perspective. For example, it is much worse to

believe that someone you love is about to fall gravely ill than it is to experience the feeling while simultaneously knowing that the feeling is not a true vision of the future, but rather is your way of responding to "too much" pleasure or to a disappointment. As you increasingly become able to keep painful moods in perspective, that is, as you become aware that you turn to them for a kind of comfort in certain circumstances, they will become less and less convincing and, therefore, not so overwhelming.

- *Once you can keep your painful feelings in context, you are well on the road to recovery.* You will have the dual experience of suffering from a painful mood while your "normal" self remains functional and able to keep the painful mood contained. Eventually, the depression, anxiety, or irritability will feel less like an avalanche that is burying you, and more like an annoyance, such as a mild headache, which you know will pass and which can be largely ignored. One day you will find that the painful moods that plagued you are hardly even showing up on your radar screen.

In the pages that follow, we offer specific strategies to help you follow these guidelines and to turn away from the familiar comfort of gratuitous unhappiness.

## Knowing the Difference Between Appropriate Unhappiness and Gratuitous (Self-Caused) Unhappiness

Because your emotions have such a profound effect on your experience of yourself and the world, they feel completely real. And they are real in the sense that you truly feel "that way." But that does not mean that you lack the power to choose to feel otherwise. As we have said, there are two kinds of emotions: emotions that are appropriate responses to life events, and emotions that, usually without realizing it, you cause yourself. Appropriate emotions may be positive or negative. For example, falling in love will feel positive, but hearing that you are being laid off will obviously feel negative.

If children's emotional needs are adequately met, then when those children become adults, their *self-caused* emotions will be only positive and never negative. As adults, they will always feel loveable, loving, and loved. They will never turn to depression or other painful feelings as a source of comfort and well-being. On the other hand, if children's emotional needs are not met and they consequently confuse unhappiness with happiness and learn to feel good by feeling bad, then when these children become adults, they will sometimes cause themselves unpleasant emotions, or gratuitous unhappiness.

The prerequisite for freeing yourself from painful moods is to learn to distinguish appropriate unhappiness from gratuitous unhappiness. Some people like to keep a daily record of their emotions; others can't be bothered. It really doesn't matter how you do it, but it is important to begin to notice the degree to which your unhappiness is gratuitous, that is, self-caused. For example, if you have had a loss or disappointment, you will naturally feel some degree of sadness, but you may also have painful feelings that are out of proportion to the loss you have experienced. These feelings represent gratuitous unhappiness.

The following guidelines can help you to distinguish appropriate from gratuitous unhappiness:

## Appropriate Unhappiness

- Is always the direct result of a genuinely upsetting event (i.e., illness or death of a loved one, loss of a desired job, or failure to get a sought-for promotion).
- Includes disappointed or sad feelings and, in the case of some severe losses, may also include nonspecific angry feelings.
- Does not include severely self-critical feelings, ongoing depression, unprovoked anger at others, a state of blankness, or unfounded fears or anxieties.

### Gratuitous Unhappiness

- Can include harsh feelings toward oneself, chronic depression, a state of blankness, or unfounded fears, anxiety, suspicion, or anger.
- May piggyback on a real loss. An example is a man we know who discovered that his hearing had deteriorated. In addition to the sadness appropriate to learning he had become hard of hearing, he was overcome by feelings of shame at the thought of wearing a hearing aid. As a result, he didn't follow up and get the hearing aid, and he suffered the frustration of being unable to hear well in social situations.
- Does not necessarily have any connection to an upsetting event. Gratuitous unhappiness may follow good feelings or simply appear "out of nowhere."

### Knowing Yourself: Identifying How and When You Experience Gratuitous Unhappiness.

First identify the kind of gratuitous unhappiness that causes you the most distress. Perhaps you are most troubled by feeling "down," or you are bothered by anxious thoughts or feelings you can't shake, or you feel unaccountably irritable. You may be all too aware of the kind of gratuitous unhappiness that plagues you. For example, you may be terrified of flying or terribly anxious whenever you have to speak in front of people. Or your particular kind of gratuitous unhappiness may have been invisible because it has existed as a kind of "background noise" of anxiety, depression, fuzziness, or self-criticism. By focusing on this background discomfort, you can begin to notice its presence or absence.

Once you have identified the negative feelings that are interfering in your life, keep track of when they occur. Perhaps, like a fear of flying or public speaking, they are stimulated by a particular activity. Other feelings may seem to come out of nowhere. Or maybe they are most likely to descend on you after you have been feeling especially good or after you have had a disappointment you weren't expecting. As you go through your day, take your emotional temperature. For example, if you are feeling happy and satisfied, notice if and when these positive feelings are replaced by negative emotions. Keep up your observations until a pattern emerges.

## Jill

*Jill was a history teacher who was plagued by bouts of feeling "down." While she was able to grit her teeth and keep going, these depressed feelings took a lot out of her. Worst of all, she could never predict when she would feel bad because the feelings seemed to come and go randomly. As a result, she felt helpless and could not enjoy good feelings when she had them because she had no idea when they would be replaced by depressed feelings.*

*Jill was resigned to living a life that periodically felt oppressive until she learned about the addiction to unhappiness. Once she understood that without realizing it she was feeling blue because she had long ago confused this painful feeling with happiness, she immediately felt less helpless. She began to keep a diary of her "unpleasant" feelings. She noted how she had been feeling before the "down" feelings occurred and also how long they lasted.*

*Much to her surprise Jill discovered that there was a definite pattern to her depressions. They always occurred shortly after she was feeling happy about something. In fact, the better she was feeling, the more depressed she became and the longer the depression lasted.*

*Once Jill identified this pattern, she thought back and saw that it had always been there. The day after her marriage, she had felt so out-of-sorts that she had told her husband that she was ill in order to explain to him why she couldn't be more affectionate. She realized that after a day in which her classes had gone well and she felt pride in her teaching and delighted with her students' progress, on the drive home she would dwell on aspects of her life that weren't perfect and would arrive home feeling dissatisfied and irritable. At the same time, she noticed that when her day went badly—she lost her temper in class, or a lesson did not go as she had planned—she usually felt on an even keel all the way home.*

*Armed with this knowledge, Jill began to notice when she was feeling happy. She knew this meant that she needed to be on the lookout for an aversive reaction to her good feelings. Sometimes just knowing that the addiction to unhappiness was going to tempt her to restore the familiar feelings of unhappiness kept the depression at bay. Even when she did feel blue, she was usually prepared. Because the feelings made sense to her and were expected, they did not feel so overwhelming and she no longer felt helpless.*

## Looking Ahead: Anticipating Gratuitous Unhappiness

Once you have identified both the emotions that most trouble you and the experiences that are likely to trigger them, you can begin to work on anticipating or predicting unpleasant emotions before they occur. The key is to become much more attuned to your emotional state and how it fluctuates.

If you are a person who tends to overreact to negative experiences by heaping on painful feelings of self-criticism, guilt, depression, or anxiety, you can learn to be especially watchful when something goes wrong—for example, when you hit a roadblock at work, lose a game, or break something.

### Pat

*Pat worked in an office with coworkers who seemed to find endless enjoyment in being critical of fellow officemates behind their backs. Typically, Pat would have an enjoyable lunch with an officemate she considered a friend. Subsequently, she would hear that the "friend" had said something negative about her. Pat would react by dwelling on the* negative comment and feeling exposed and terribly upset. Sometimes it would be a day or two before she could regain her inner equilibrium.

As a result of working with us, Pat learned that the most painful part of the unhappiness she was feeling was not the result of being betrayed by someone she thought of as a friend but came from the self-caused pain she turned to as a way of handling the disappointment.

She recalled, "As far back as I can remember, whenever something went wrong—I broke a toy or tripped and scraped my knee—my parents found some way to make me feel responsible. One time when my boyfriend dumped me for my best friend, my parents actually said it was my fault because I hadn't worked hard enough at making him happy!" Pat could see that she had copied her parents' misguided attempts to help her cope with loss and had learned to find "comfort" in self-critical feelings.

Armed with this understanding, Pat became better at identifying and anticipating the feelings of shame and depression she turned to when she felt betrayed. After an all-day series of meetings she attended with a coworker, Alicia, Pat was told by another colleague that Alicia had complained that "Pat puts on airs and acts like she's the boss." Pat was immediately able to say to herself, "Before I make myself feel terrible, let me think about this." She realized that Alicia was probably envious because Pat had made excellent suggestions at the meeting and their boss had commented favorably on her input. By anticipating her self-critical reaction to Alicia's negative comment, Pat was able to fend it off long enough to diffuse it with a healthy dose of reality.

Pat increasingly found that by anticipating the waves of depression and shame that inundated her whenever she heard a negative comment, she could hold these painful emotions to a manageable level.

If you are a person who has unknowingly learned to respond to disappointment by feeling self-critical, unloveable, anxious, irritable, muddled, helpless, or depressed, you too can learn to say to yourself the moment you experience a loss, "The next thing that will happen is that

I will feel a black cloud descending on me." Sometimes just getting the jump on gratuitous unhappiness will keep it at bay, but even if it envelops you, you will be prepared and not taken by surprise. This will give you the leverage necessary to weaken the power gratuitous unhappiness has over your life. The knowledge that you have anticipated it, and that it is a familiar but nonadaptive way of soothing yourself when things go wrong, can keep this unhappiness from swamping you and allow you to remain connected to the mind you had before the gratuitous unhappiness occurred. That is, you can learn to keep your bearings and to avoid agreeing with the voice that says you are blameworthy or guilty and then sinking into feelings of depression or anxiety.

Perhaps when you identify the painful emotions you cause yourself, you will discover that you are a person who tends to feel miserable in reaction to positive experiences. In this case, good rather than bad experiences will become the occasion for anticipating gratuitous unhappiness.

### *James*

*As long as he could remember, James intermittently suffered from the conviction that he was a "bad" person. This feeling was very painful, and when it was at its height it was difficult for James to function effectively in relationships and at work. James felt like a "failure" in spite of the fact that he had a good job as a set designer and was in a committed relationship with a woman he loved. James' belief that he was "no good" seemed like a guilty secret that would inevitably become public.*

*When he became acquainted with our work and learned that his negative feelings about himself were a manifestation of the addiction to unhappiness, that is, that he was causing them even though he certainly wasn't consciously choosing them, James began to feel hopeful. Previously his feelings of worthlessness had come and gone seemingly without rhyme or reason. He never knew from day to day if he would feel relatively all right, or whether he would be haunted by feelings of* worthlessness. Once he knew that without realizing it he was the author of all his feelings, his sense of helplessness began to diminish.

James kept a careful diary to track when his self-critical feelings appeared. He had expected that they would follow times when he "screwed up." To his surprise, he found that when things went wrong he was able to maintain his inner equilibrium. He was amazed to discover that his feelings of being "no good" nearly always descended when he was feeling happy and satisfied. He noticed that he suffered through a particularly painful siege of feeling "no good" after he moved into a new and much nicer apartment.

Now James could see why his painful moods always seemed to come out of nowhere. His feelings of worthlessness were not tied in any way to reality. Rather they were aversive reactions to feeling happy. "Too much" pleasure deprived him of the familiar comfort he got from disliking himself and stimulated him to re-create these "good" feelings. Armed with this information, James carefully noted when things were going particularly well and when he was feeling happy and satisfied. Then he watched for the first sign of feeling that he was a "bad" person. When they arose, James labeled these painful emotions as a reaction to feeling happy, and he ceased to be persuaded by them. Although there were times when James was taken by surprise and found himself feeling terrible, overall, his feelings of worthlessness continued to lose power. James was finally able to enjoy the good life he had worked so hard to create.

## Two Steps Forward, One Step Back: The Course of Genuine Progress

We do not mean to give the impression that the course of liberating yourself from the addiction to painful emotions will proceed smoothly. We have been emphasizing that you can get control, but we know that the process may be neither easy nor straightforward. As with all improvements to your life, the need for the familiar comfort of unhappiness you have unknowingly confused with happiness can assert itself the moment that you begin to try to wean yourself from it.

The difficulties may arise around getting started. You may find it difficult to keep your diary of emotions or in general to notice when pleasant feelings are replaced by painful ones. If at first you find it too difficult to remain aware of your emotions throughout the day, pick a time frame that is more doable. For example, notice how you feel for the first hour after you wake up. Try taking your emotional temperature at the beginning of every hour and see how long you can remain aware of it. Even if days go by and you haven't been able to zero in on your feelings, keep trying. The addiction to unhappiness may stimulate you to believe that you have missed your chance or that you aren't up to it. None of this is true. You can be in the beginning phase for as long as necessary. Even if you can pay attention to how you are feeling only for five minutes now and then, you are making progress. *No effort is too little or too late.*

Once you have gotten through the information-gathering phase and know what kind of painful emotions trouble you most and when they are most likely to appear, the next stage is to anticipate them. To do this, you need to be on the lookout for specific feelings or experiences you have identified as triggering painful states of mind. Triggering experiences precede bouts of emotional pain. They range from disappointment at a loss, to happiness at success, to a sense of inner well-being that has remained stable for a while.

This anticipation stage is another time when you may find your resolve weakening. You may find it difficult to remember to watch for the triggering emotion and then find yourself feeling miserable without having any idea why. After a few more missed connections, you may be tempted to conclude that the task of anticipating bouts of emotional pain is too much work or that it is beyond your capacity.

The key is not to burden yourself with unreasonable expectations. You need to keep in mind that you are trying to unlearn a way of feeling inner comfort that you have turned to since you were a child. This way of soothing yourself may not disappear quickly or easily, but you can wean yourself from it if you keep trying. Any kind of progress will eventually get you where you are going. If you only notice a triggering emotion and anticipate painful moods once every week or once a month, over time you will still succeed.

The next pitfall to be aware of is the tendency to become discouraged and to give up when you backslide. As we have emphasized, lapses are part of the healing process. They are a form of aversive reaction to genuine pleasure: the addiction to unhappiness reasserts itself in reaction to the pleasure you feel at the progress you have made. Backsliding follows success. The addiction to unhappiness may try to make you believe that if you backslide, you cannot accomplish your goal.

### Kenneth

*Kenneth, a 45-year-old engineer, was tormented by the fear of coming down with terminal cancer. He was subject to vivid fantasies in which he got the bad news, said goodbye to friends and family, and never had the chance to enjoy his hard-won accomplishments.*

*Once he knew that his fear was an expression of the addiction to unhappiness, Kenneth identified the triggering emotion as the pleasure he felt when he worked hard for a goal and achieved it. He noticed that when he successfully completed a large and complex engineering project and took a few days off to relax, he was overcome with the conviction that he had cancer. In effect the anxiety about dying was undoing his good feelings about his accomplishment because it conveyed the message, "It doesn't matter what I have achieved, I will die soon and never be able to reap the benefits of my hard work."*

*Kenneth worked hard to notice when he was feeling good about an achievement. Then he anticipated that he would immediately react with gloomy thoughts of dying. Once he predicted the occurrence of these painful feelings, they took him less by surprise and seemed much less authentic.*

*Kenneth felt increasingly effective and in charge of his emotions. Because he no longer spent so much of his time focused on dying, he was freer to enjoy living. Then an old friend was diagnosed with cancer. Kenneth immediately convinced himself that his optimism had been for nothing, and that any day he, too, would get the fatal diagnosis.*

*Kenneth's fears were stronger than ever, and no amount of anticipation seemed to blunt their influence on him. As we worked with him, Kenneth began to see that although his friend's cancer seemed like "proof" that his fears were well-founded, in fact his addiction to unhappiness had seized on this coincidence to reassert itself and regain lost ground. Kenneth began to understand that the resurgence in his fears was less about his friend's illness than it was an aversive reaction to the pleasure of feeling happier. At that point, his determination to get the best of his addiction to unhappiness rebounded, and his fears became much less persuasive. Furthermore, the next episode of backsliding did not take him so completely by surprise and he recovered from it much more quickly.*

The last snare on the way to recovering from the addiction to painful emotions is the tendency to let your guard down when you have succeeded in distancing yourself from the painful moods that have been so troubling. No matter how much better you feel, it is important to think of yourself not as cured, but as a recovering addict to painful emotions. In this way, if unpleasant emotions manage to insinuate themselves back into your life, you will not be surprised or conclude that your progress has not been real. Rather you will be expecting that your depression, anxiety, or fears will reappear once in a while. Because by this time you will have had so much success at marginalizing these feelings, you will find that if you are on the lookout for them, you can dispel them and return to the positive feelings that are your birthright.

## When to Seek Professional Help

Among the various expressions of the addiction to unhappiness, the addiction to painful emotions is the hardest to cure. The reason is that emotions by their nature feel imposed and not chosen. It can be very difficult to believe that we are the authors of our emotions and even harder to get control over our emotional choices. When the addiction to unhappiness involves a physical action, such as overeating or provoking verbal fights with loved ones, it is much easier to see that we are causing our own unhappiness and to know what to do to feel happier (i.e., eat less or censor those provocative comments).

While we know from experience that the guidelines and strategies outlined in this chapter can help most people, we also know that some individuals whose early years were particularly unhappy and difficult develop a particularly resistant type of addiction to painful emotions. These individuals may need professional assistance to get control of their emotional pain. If you have repeatedly tried to follow the guidelines in this chapter but find that you either cannot anticipate self-caused emotional pain or cannot get any perspective on it when it occurs (with the result that it continues to overwhelm you), you may need the assistance of a caring professional. In choosing this person, it is important to look for someone who understands that individuals can learn to regulate their own mind experience and to be in charge of their emotions, and who never makes clients feel helpless or ashamed of having emotional pain, no matter what form it takes.

# Chapter 5

# Conquering Your Resistance to Achieving Physical Well-Being

I f you are one of the many people who find it difficult to maintain a healthy weight, to keep fit, and generally to take care of your body, you may have concluded that you lack will power. For example, you may have found that no matter what diet or exercise program you begin, you run out of steam somewhere along the line. What you probably didn't know is that you were being swayed by an unseen influence. Your inability to maintain your weight or to keep to an exercise program was not due to any weakness of character, but to the heretofore unrecognized addiction to unhappiness. When you don't take good care of your body, the addiction to unhappiness is satisfied in two ways. You suffer the unpleasant consequences of ill health, injuries, or being unfit. You also experience the self-critical feelings (unhappiness) that come from letting your body be hurt, unwell, over- or underweight, or unfit. An example is the woman who couldn't lose weight and accepted that she would inevitably feel unhappy as long as she was "fat."

There are any number of ways in which the caregiving children receive can interfere with their ability to care for their bodies as adults. For example, when parents are overly concerned that children eat well and force them to eat when they are not hungry, children may copy this approach to food. As adults, instead of ceasing to eat when they are no longer hungry, they may feel false pleasure (unhappiness in disguise) when they go on to clean their plates.

Or when parents express anger by handling children roughly, children may copy parents and learn to treat their own bodies with anger or indifference. As adults, these children may be careless, neglectful, or even actively destructive of their physical well-being. On the other hand, when parents are permissive, that is, fail to protect their children adequately from their immaturity, children often have frequent accidents and injuries. They may develop an addiction to the unhappiness of putting themselves at risk and hurting themselves, which they experience as normal.

## Why Diet and Exercise Are Harder Than They Should Be

Difficulty maintaining a healthy body is one of the most common forms of the addiction to unhappiness probably because many parents, who have responsibility for the care and feeding of their children's bodies from birth, are sometimes loving and sometimes unintentionally either too rough or too permissive. Many adults relate to their bodies in ways that cause pain as well as pleasure. For example, the genuine pleasure of eating nutritious food becomes entangled with the false pleasure (unhappiness in disguise) of eating mostly unhealthy foods or eating too much. Eating feels like comfort that can't be had any other way, which makes it difficult to stop. In fact, overeating is one of the best ways to illustrate that the unhappiness to which people can become addicted is a false pleasure that has been confused with true pleasure. (In eating disorders, of course, the false pleasure consists of the illusion of control that comes from eating too little, or eating and purging.)

Similarly, many people don't get the exercise they need because they feel it is less pleasurable than alternative activities such as reading, napping, watching TV, or surfing the Internet. Exercise feels like a burden, whereas sedentary activities feel relaxing and pleasurable. This, too, is an instance in which a pleasure (relaxing) is carried to an extreme because it is being driven by an unrecognized need for unhappiness.

A variant of this problem is the difficulty many people experience when they are told by their doctor that their health requires that they eat a restricted diet of some kind or that they strengthen their cardiovascular system through exercise. People often experience the prescribed regimen as unpleasant and long for the forbidden foods or the sedentary state they have always "enjoyed." In reality, of course, the desire for foods and a lifestyle that jeopardize one's health is an expression of the addiction to unhappiness.

There are also people who don't exercise because they believe that they are so fat or out of shape that it would be horribly embarrassing to go to the gym or to be seen outside walking or jogging. These feelings of shame are inspired by the addiction to unhappiness that prevents the individual from pursuing the genuine pleasure of becoming healthier.

The addiction to unhappiness can lead people to sabotage their diets or exercise programs by choosing methods that are unsafe. These people may harm (and sometimes even kill) themselves in the misguided belief that they are taking care of themselves. Examples are people who take diet drugs that interact dangerously with their other medications; people who undertake extremely unbalanced diets (such as all protein) for long periods of time; people who starve themselves in the name of dieting; and people who suddenly begin exercising vigorously without first getting a medical checkup.

The addiction to unhappiness can also interfere with a person's physical well-being by causing aversive reactions to the possibility of looking and feeling good. The genuine pleasure of feeling healthy interferes with the pain of being overweight or unfit, which had been satisfying the addiction to unhappiness by feeling comfortable and, therefore, pleasant. An individual may try to recapture that false pleasure by abandoning a diet or an exercise plan.

## Arthur

Arthur's addiction to unhappiness made it impossible for him to maintain a program of healthy physical exercise. Usually when he began to experience the genuine pleasure of physical well-being, he stopped exercising, overate, and gained weight. Eventually, Arthur became so frustrated that he consulted us.

Arthur grew up in a family with two busy working parents. In the process of managing two careers, running a house, and taking care of four children, Arthur's parents didn't always manage to pay attention to Arthur's physical needs. He frequently missed regular dental and medical checkups, no one noticed if he brushed his teeth, and because his parents had little extra time for playing, he spent much of his free time sitting and watching TV. Arthur, of course, didn't understand that his parents were overwhelmed with responsibilities and were not intentionally neglecting his physical well-being. He grew up addicted to the false pleasure (unhappiness masquerading as happiness) of being sedentary and of ignoring his needs for exercise.

We helped Arthur to see that each time he began to exercise, he reacted to the pleasure of becoming fit with unrecognized needs to make himself unhappy. As a result, he began to anticipate times of resistance. When he found it difficult to get out of bed after three straight days of exercising, he recognized that the problem was less that he was tired than that he was trying to rob himself of sustained healthy pleasure by substituting the false pleasure (unhappiness) of not taking care of his body. Rather than rebuking himself for lacking willpower and being lazy, as he had previously done, he planned to head off his need to sabotage his exercise program. For example, he saved his favorite form of exercise for later in the week. When he felt serious resistance coming on, he called a friend and made a date to go running together. Sometimes he still missed a planned exercise day, but over time he became more and more consistent. Just as pleasurable as his increased physical well-being was his realization that he could make his life go the way he wished.

Once you realize that unhealthy foods or a sedentary lifestyle are not offering you a genuine type of pleasure, but actually satisfy a need to mistreat your body you long ago confused with happiness, you will have taken the first step toward turning away from this false soothing.

## Jeopardizing Your Physical Well-Being

While the influence of the addiction to unhappiness on the body is often obvious, as when a person is seriously overweight, is allowing obvious health problems to go untreated, or is drinking too much, sometimes the operation of the addiction to unhappiness can be disguised. With this in mind, consider whether you sometimes put your physical well-being in jeopardy. For example, there are people who feel comfortable and even exhilarated when they take significant risks, such as driving or skiing too fast for conditions. Others engage in risky behaviors without realizing it or in the belief that they are somehow exempt from harm. They climb ladders that aren't adequately secured, hike without proper equipment or without telling anyone where they have gone, fail to protect themselves from the sun's rays, have unsafe sex, or put off long overdue medical exams, such as mammograms or prostate tests.

### Peter

*Peter was a hard-charging executive who played as hard as he worked and who loved challenges. He was a strong swimmer, and one of his favorite pastimes was swimming in ocean surf—the bigger the waves, the better he liked them. When there was a storm and the Coast Guard posted no-swimming warnings, he would ignore them. He told his wife that those were his favorite days to swim because he found the mammoth waves "exhilarating." When his wife would beg him not to go in the water at times when swimming was prohibited, he became irritable and accused her of infantilizing him. He reminded her of how hard he worked and said angrily that he had a right to any recreation he chose. Peter had absolutely no clue that the risks he was running were not in the service of genuine fun but were attractive because putting himself in danger gratified the addiction to unhappiness.*

*As a young child, Peter had been allowed to run along the top of walls, bike without a helmet, and play with older children who were rough and frequently injured him. His parents had believed that restraints would compromise Peter's athletic promise and make a "sissy" of him. Naturally enough, Peter himself had become addicted to the false happiness (unhappiness) generated by living "on the edge."*

*Finally, courting danger caught up with Peter. Once again he had ignored a Coast Guard ban on swimming. He dove through one huge wave, only to find that there was an even bigger wave right behind it. This wave smashed him into the sand, breaking a number of ribs, dislocating his shoulder, and giving him a serious concussion. During his lengthy recuperation, Peter, considerably shaken, took seriously his wife's suggestion that he get professional help to discover why he found it so pleasurable to place himself in significant danger.*

## Taking Inventory: Deciding What Needs to Change

The first step in improving your weight, health, fitness level, and general self-care is to decide what aspect of your physical well-being you want to work on first. Some people find that they can only tolerate concentrating on one aspect of their behavior at a time (for example, dieting saps all their energy). Others find it easier and more effective to combine projects (for example, they may decide to cut back on alcohol consumption, diet, and begin exercising all at one time). There is no one best way to proceed. *Most important is any sort of forward motion.* And if you think you will succeed best by taking on two or three problems at once but find that you begin to feel overwhelmed, you can always cut back and concentrate on one thing at a time.

We suggest that you take an inventory of your physical condition, including activities you have categorized as "lifestyle choices" (e.g., riding your bike without a helmet) to see whether the addiction to unhappiness is affecting you in ways that you don't recognize, as well as in ways you have been only too aware of. Some categories you may find it helpful to consider are fitness, eating habits, level of alcohol consumption, smoking, risk taking, and arranging for adequate medical attention.

One common error in assessing your physical well-being is to miss current problems by assuming you are in the same physical condition as when you were much younger.

### Kevin

*Kevin had been a superstar in college basketball. Throughout his childhood and until he entered law school, he was always in superb physical condition. He could run up and down the steps of a football stadium for half an hour without breathing hard. During law school and the years he spent becoming a partner in the law firm he joined, Kevin worked long hours and almost never got a chance to exercise. He gave no thought to staying fit, because the addiction to unhappiness blinded him to the possibility that his body could ever get out of shape. Kevin didn't realize it, but his failure to stay fit was actually an aversive reaction to the pleasure of the superb physical condition and athletic success he had attained in high school and college. In his second year out of law school, Kevin married and, shortly thereafter, had two children.*

*As a father, a husband, and an attorney with a busy practice, he never seemed to find time for exercising, but he continued to think of himself as a star athlete who didn't happen to be exercising. Shortly after his forty-fifth birthday, there was an enormous snowstorm and Kevin went out with his son to shovel his driveway. An hour later he experienced chest pains. His doctor said that he was so out of shape that shoveling snow caused his heart muscle to demand oxygen that the blood vessels to his heart couldn't supply. Fortunately, when he experienced pain Kevin sought treatment immediately and there was no permanent damage to his heart muscle. Kevin was shocked by the news that he was so out of shape. He responded to this wake-up call by making time every morning for the exercise program his doctor prescribed and supervised.*

As you assess how you are treating your body, be on the lookout for harmful activities that appear innocuous or, even, beneficial. For example, a surprising number of people overexercise. This aspect of the addiction to unhappiness is often difficult to notice, because people are convinced that more is better. If running five miles a day for five days is good for you, the thinking goes, then running seven miles a day for seven days must be better. Often even an injury fails to alert these individuals to the existence of a problem; they often go right back to overexercising as soon as they are healed.

Warning signs of overexercising include the following: You keep stepping up your idea of how much exercise you should do daily; you never or rarely take a day off from exercising; you exercise more than you want to in order to work off food you didn't mean to eat; you don't feel you have exercised enough unless you feel exhausted at the end of your workout; and you don't listen to your body—you stick to your exercise program even when you wake up feeling ill, bone tired, or in considerable pain. This is another instance of how the addiction to unhappiness can transform a genuine pleasure (keeping fit) into unhappiness in disguise (exercising to the point of hurting yourself).

Other kinds of activities to consider in your assessment of how you are treating your body are those that are not manifestly injurious but carry an unaccountably high probability of harm. You may feel the dangerous activity is acceptable because you believe you will beat the odds, but in effect you are satisfying the addiction to unhappiness by playing Russian roulette with your health. Examples of unacceptable high-risk activities are driving too fast or when tired, unsafe sex, operating power tools without adequate precautions or instruction, and not wearing a seat belt.

Another kind of high-risk behavior involves avoiding medical care. Many people regularly put off physical exams and recommended screening tests, they fail to see their doctor about worrisome symptoms, or they do not follow a prescribed regimen. They convince themselves that they are too busy or are too healthy to seek medical care, but in reality only the addiction to unhappiness would cause them to take chances with something as important to their overall happiness as their health.

## Identifying Potential Trouble Spots Before You Begin Your Self-Improvement Program

Once you have identified the aspects of your health and fitness you want to change and are ready to begin your self-improvement program, take a moment to consider when and how the addiction to unhappiness derailed your past efforts. For example, maybe you couldn't get started, or you stopped after a few weeks. Or you made tremendous improvements and then slid back to square one or below. If you can, write down your daily, weekly, and monthly goals and mark the past trouble spots in red so that you are prepared to redouble your efforts when you reach them.

### *Recognizing the Problem*

One way the addiction to unhappiness can undermine your good intentions to become healthy and fit is to allow you to downplay the problem once it is identified, with the result that correcting the problem begins to seem optional. Since the addiction to unhappiness is likely to make the cure feel burdensome, convincing yourself that the problem isn't serious makes it easy to postpone or abandon efforts to fix it. A man we know could not take seriously the 30 pounds he was overweight until his cholesterol level became seriously elevated.

Once you have identified those aspects of your physical condition that need changing, keep an eye out for the temptation to dismiss the problem as minor. Put differently, thoughts that tell you it is OK to be overweight or unfit are not genuinely soothing, but are silently driven by needs to make yourself unhappy. Ask yourself whether, if you had a real choice, you would ever choose to jeopardize your health by remaining in poor physical shape. The answer, of course, is No. The reason for your struggle is that being overweight or unfit feels familiar and comforting, that is, being less than healthy satisfies the addiction to unhappiness.

A variant of downplaying risks to your health is to recognize that they are *potentially* harmful, but not to take the risk seriously because you are convinced that you will change your behavior in time—before the risks "get you." Smoking is a good example. Many smokers have in mind some number of years that they will allow themselves to smoke before they have to quit. These may be loosely based on risk tables they have seen. Or they plan to smoke until the first signs of a health problem appear, such as emphysema or abnormal cells in throat or mouth. They have the illusion of being in control when in fact an addiction to unhappiness is running the show.

People who drink too much are also prone to believing that they are choosing to drink—that they can stop whenever they want, but that the time hasn't come yet. The same is true of many other risk takers. They tell themselves that they will begin to wear a bike helmet when it's not so hot out or that they will ski more slowly after the passing of a few more birthdays. These people also are convinced that they are in charge of their lives even though in reality they are captives of an addiction to unhappiness. This fact becomes obvious the moment this question is posed: Why would anyone who had a true choice postpone giving up the false pleasure of potentially harmful behavior when they could enjoy the genuine pleasure of taking the best possible care of their bodies?

## Other Potential Trouble Spots

Perhaps during past efforts at self-improvement you were able to identify the problem you wanted to change, but you found it very difficult to get started. As we described in the introduction to this section, setting a start date in the future can convey an illusory sense of forward motion that temporarily dissipates when the start date passes but is renewed when a new start date is set. Some people go for years resolving that at the beginning of the next week or the next month they will make the changes they know to be in their best interest.

Other problem areas to be aware of are losing momentum or, even, sliding back to square one or beyond after making a promising start. Try to identify your state of mind when you lost ground: perhaps you felt the effort was too much for you or you went down fighting or you didn't realize you were giving up because you thought you were just taking a break.

Finally, maybe you reached your goal and lowered your guard only to find that the addiction to unhappiness regained strength and the pounds you lost crept back, you gradually stopped exercising, you started speeding again, and so on.

Even if one or more of these pitfalls trapped you on your previous attempts to improve your physical well-being, identifying them will help you succeed in your next effort. Knowing which siren song is most likely to cause you to stray from your chosen path will make it easier to plug your ears and keep forging ahead when you hear it the next time.

## Strategies for Getting in Shape

Once you have identified the problem you want to correct and the obstacles that the addiction to unhappiness is likely to throw in your path, you are ready to begin. *Keep in mind that your new awareness of potential roadblocks is not a cure.* You are still going to have to do battle with your learned need for unhappiness (for example, it may be necessary to blast through stubborn resistance, the apparent disappearance of all positive motivation, and thoughts of being unequal to the task), and you will no doubt lose some skirmishes. You are, however, poised to win the war.

## Get Ready to Start . . . and Begin

You know what you want to accomplish (lose 10 pounds, exercise for 30 minutes five times a week, stop smoking, drive more slowly) and you are ready to get started. The getting started phase is easy for some people and hard for others. If you are a person for whom getting started is easy, you will simply pick a date and begin. For the moment we are speaking to those of you who have trouble beginning.

*Choose a start date that is no more than three days away.* If you choose a date that is farther away, you will simply put the project out of your mind until the last three days.

*As the start date approaches, prepare for an internal fight.* You may begin to feel that it's too difficult right now because you have houseguests, you are swamped at work, you are going on a business trip, etc. You may start to think the project isn't necessary now because you aren't really as overweight as most people you know; you haven't exercised in so long that a little more time won't matter; you can't restrict your salt as the doctor recommended because you are going to be eating in so many restaurants; it's too hot to start exercising in the summer, and fall would be a better time to think about it. You may discover that the resolve you had three days ago has quietly disappeared, or there may be some other reason why it makes more sense to postpone beginning.

*Discount your reasons for not starting ahead of time.* Decide up front that no matter what arguments present themselves for postponing your efforts to improve your physical well-being, you are not going to listen. In effect plug your ears to temptation and concentrate on combating your internal resistance. When a salesman who was consulting us planned a diet and then had to make a business trip, he immediately began to feel that there was no point in starting because he would be eating airplane and hotel food for five days. Rather than give in to this feeling, which he knew was prompted by the addiction to unhappiness, he located a book that focused on dieting while traveling and began his diet on the day he had chosen.

*Realize that starting may never feel easy, and try to keep in mind that achieving your goal is worth some discomfort now.* Buy a beautiful dress or suit in the size you want to be, or plan to treat yourself to a fun activity like a weekend bike trip when you get fit.

*Keep in mind that the struggle you are going through is the result of the addiction to unhappiness rather than because it is inherently difficult or unpleasant to improve your level of physical well-being.* A man who was seeing us concluded after a number of failed attempts to begin exercising regularly that he couldn't get started because exercising was so difficult and unpleasant. He needed help to realize that in reality the unpleasantness he experienced was the result of his addiction to the unhappiness of being unfit. When he finally managed to start exercising regularly, he found to his surprise that he actually enjoyed it.

*If in spite of all your efforts you let the start date go by, do not let yourself be convinced that you are too weak or unmotivated to succeed. Set another start date and try again.*

*When you succeed in starting, immediately do something genuinely nice for yourself.* A woman we know promised herself a massage the day she started her diet.

## Sticking with It

No matter what aspect of your physical well-being you choose to improve, as soon as you start to make changes, you may find your determination flagging. The diet or exercise program may seem like too much work, you may lose touch with the reason that convinced you it was time to make a change, or you may find yourself renegotiating with yourself. For example, if you set out to lose 10 pounds, you may be tempted to stop at 5 pounds; if you have promised yourself to drive the speed limit, you may feel that you need to drive fast "this time" because you are late.

If you know that as soon as you start to improve your physical well-being the addiction to unhappiness can cause your resolve to waver, you will be more prepared to turn a deaf ear to the negative voices telling you it's too hard, it's not worth it, or you chose too ambitious a goal.

Remember that no matter how attractive a particular choice may seem, you need to ask yourself whether it is in the service of creating genuine pleasure or of causing yourself unhappiness that you long ago confused with happiness. This will make it easier to resist the conviction that you would feel better if you salted your potatoes even though you have high blood pressure, if you read a book instead of doing your planned exercising, or if you had unsafe sex.

### Denise

*Denise was one of those people who constantly lost and then gained back pounds. When she got to a weight that horrified her, she became determined to lose weight and was able to diet successfully. When she got her weight down somewhat, she ran out of steam. Suddenly the pleasure of pizza, cookies, and ice cream seemed much more appealing than the thought of reaching her ideal weight or even of keeping off the pounds she had lost. When she ate a hamburger and French fries topped off by a large milk shake, Denise felt she was making a deliberate choice of enjoyable food over unrewarding sacrifice. In short order, Denise would put back the pounds she had worked so hard to lose and the cycle would begin again.*

*Denise never realized that the reason she thought that overindulging in fatty foods was "enjoyable" and that eating normal portions of healthy foods was a "sacrifice" was that she had confused unhappiness with genuine happiness, with the result that causing herself the unhappiness of eating too much of the wrong foods seemed more attractive* than choosing the true happiness of watching her diet and reaching a healthy weight.

Hearing about our work gave Denise her first understanding of the cycle that had trapped her for as long as she could remember. She realized that when chocolate cake began to seem more pleasurable than reaching her ideal weight, she was having an aversive reaction to the pleasure of shedding unhealthy pounds. Now when she lost weight, she immediately began to anticipate and prepare for the time when dieting would lose its appeal. When fattening foods beckoned, she knew that the addiction to unhappiness, not genuine self-caring, made them attractive, and she found it much easier to make the choice to resist and stick to her planned menu. Increasingly she became able to evaluate the quality of the choices she made to see whether they were in the service of satisfying the addiction to unhappiness or of giving her real pleasure.

One strategy for maintaining your resolve is to *enlist the help of someone close to you.* Because this person will not share your need to feel the unhappiness you long ago confused with genuine happiness, she or he will be able to give you a reality check when you feel like smoking or sleeping in on one of your exercise days. You can check in with your support person and call when your determination starts to flag.

Often just telling someone that you feel like giving up will put you back in touch with your determination to make a positive change.

### Marion

When Marion turned 55, she scheduled the physical exam she had put off for years. She did badly on the stress test her doctor gave her because she was so out of shape. Her doctor prescribed an hour of walking six days out of every seven. Marion had always hated any sort of physical activity. Her parents had prematurely aged from lack of exercise, and they had never encouraged Marion to be physically active. She had copied her parents and learned to feel happiest when she was sedentary. She never knew that this "happiness" was really the unhappiness of being unfit, to which

*she had become addicted. Marion was fond of repeating her parents' say-*
*ing: "When I feel the urge to exercise, I lie down until it passes." Now,*
*however, she realized she could no longer avoid working out.*

*Marion walked an hour a day for four days. The fifth day she only*
*walked half an hour because she overslept. The sixth day she had a busi-*
*ness breakfast at the time she normally walked and she didn't walk at*
*all that day. The next week she only walked once. By that time she was*
*ready to give up on her exercise program altogether.*

*We suggested that she call three other friends, all of whom needed*
*either to lose weight or to exercise, and that she form a walking club*
*with them. There would be safety in numbers—on any given day at*
*least one of them would be motivated to walk and could get the oth-*
*ers going. All four agreed that they would keep each other company.*
*They picked an early time every day except Sunday and penciled it into*
*their schedules. When they got tired of one route, they varied it. They*
*chatted as they walked, which made the time go by more quickly. And*
*if one of them said she was too tired, the others would remind her of*
*the deal she had made with them and do their best to get her out and*
*walking. To her great surprise, Marion found herself looking forward*
*to the daily walk with her friends. She actually felt a loss when the "day*
*off" came and often asked one of the women if she would like to walk*
*on Sunday. Marion was thrilled six months later when the stress test*
*was repeated and the benefits of her exercise program on her cardio-*
*vascular system were plain to see.*

## Don't Let a Setback Become a Defeat

The addiction to unhappiness cannot be conquered unless you are willing to put up a fight. Every attempt at self-improvement can cause a
reactive swing back to the familiar comfort of unhappiness, and
attempts to improve your physical well-being are no exception. One
common trap is to think you can coast as you near your goal (whereas
in reality success can stimulate the addiction to unhappiness and
increase your need to undermine your efforts). Perhaps the most

destructive part of backsliding is the attractiveness of the inner voice that says all is lost if you go off your diet or don't exercise for a month.

### John

John, 45, had been trying to quit smoking from the day seven years earlier when his father, a lifetime smoker, had been diagnosed with lung cancer. John had tried every possible method from gradually cutting back, to hypnotism, to a nicotine patch, to going cold turkey. With each method, however, he ran into the same problem. He would quit for a few days or weeks, and once he quit for nearly a year. But inevitably he would have a weak moment, usually when he was out with people who were smoking and he had had a drink or two. He would smoke one or two of his friends' cigarettes. His reaction was to feel that he had blown it—that all the gains he had made were now erased. His resolve melted away and, hating himself, he would buy himself a pack of cigarettes and begin smoking again.

After a friend told John that our work might help him, he made an effort to learn about the addiction to unhappiness. He realized that smoking one or two cigarettes after a few weeks or months did not mean that all was lost, but that, on the contrary, he had made such significant progress that the addiction to unhappiness was trying to reassert itself. He saw that the feeling that all was lost came from his addiction to the unhappiness represented by smoking, that is, from needs to convince himself to go back to the familiar but harmful comforts of nicotine. Once John realized that a slip here or there did not erase the progress he was making toward the goal of giving up smoking, he felt greatly relieved. When occasionally he took a cigarette from a friend, he refused to let himself believe that he couldn't stop smoking. Rather he renewed his determination to prevent as many future slips as possible. Recently, John wrote to tell us that it has been three years since he had a cigarette.

In our experience, most diets and exercise programs run aground when individuals use lapses to convince themselves that they are too weak, it's too hard, or it's all over. It's crucial when you backslide to be prepared for the feeling that you might as well give up. That feeling comes from the addiction to unhappiness, which is trying to return you to the familiar though unrecognized comfort of being overweight, unfit, or at risk. Once you understand this, you can see that in reality the wish to give up on your constructive efforts is a reaction to the progress you have made rather than natural discouragement at encountering a setback. Backsliding is part of the healing process and not a sign to you that you can't or shouldn't press on. *In other words, the paradox of setbacks is that they are indications of success, not failure.*

If you accept that lapses are both inevitable and a sign that you are recovering from the addiction to unhappiness, you can view them as opportunities for rededication to your chosen goal and as signs of progress rather than as marks of weakness or an indication of defeat.

One way to overcome setbacks is to remain vigilant: knowing that the need to sabotage your efforts will increase, not decrease with success. The knowledge that setbacks are inevitable can prevent you from being taken by surprise when they occur. Each step you take forward should be the occasion to be on the lookout for attempts to sabotage your progress. When you get on the scale at the end of a week and discover that you have lost two pounds, you can be sure that the temptation to go off your diet will increase, not decrease. The more pounds you lose, the harder you will have to struggle to stay on your diet.

Another strategy for overcoming setbacks is to use backsliding to your advantage. You can develop an entirely new approach to episodes of backsliding. You can use them as opportunities to renew your determination to improve your physical well-being. A setback shows you where your line of defense against the addiction to unhappiness was weak and gives you the chance to strengthen it.

For example, if you have successfully managed to give up alcohol for a few months but then you go to a wedding and find yourself drinking down one toast after another, rather than conclude that you have fallen off the wagon and you may as well forget about trying to remain sober, you can determine that this particular slip will not happen again. The next time you can prepare for the temptation that caught you the last time. At the next wedding or big party plan to be more vigilant. If you come to your table to find alcohol already poured, get rid of it before you sit down. Most important, go to the wedding or party anticipating that the struggle not to drink will be harder there. If it helps, think of something to substitute for alcohol (get out on the dance floor, find someone to talk to).

If you know that setbacks provide you with the opportunity to grow stronger and to be more vigilant, they can seem more like vaccines (protection against future lapses) than like failures.

## Reaping the Benefit of the Gains You've Made

One of the most effective traps the addiction to unhappiness can spring on you is to lull you into thinking that because you have achieved the goal of improving your physical well-being, you no longer have to struggle to preserve your gains. It frequently occurs that people who have reached their ideal weight, become fit, stopped smoking, or reduced their cholesterol level by careful eating become overconfident, and they cease to pay attention. However, because the addiction to unhappiness remains potent and may even be strengthened by being deprived of its usual portion of false happiness, it can come roaring back. Before a person realizes it, the pounds are back on, the exercise equipment is gathering dust, the ashtrays are in use, and the cholesterol level is climbing.

So when you reach your goal, maintain or even increase your vigilance. It bears repeating that you need to continue to think of yourself as a recovering addict to unhappiness. And if you slip, do not listen to the voice that says all your effort was for nothing and you should give up. It is not surprising that the addiction to unhappiness can still trip you up from time to time. But because you have succeeded, you know that you have the ability to reclaim the level of physical well-being you reached before.

You should remain vigilant to some of the common tricks the addiction to unhappiness can play on you after you have succeeded in reaching your goal:

- *The bargaining-with-yourself time bomb.* On the way to your goal, as a way of keeping your resolve, you may be tempted to make Faustian bargains with yourself that hold out the promise that you can indulge yourself once you reach your goal (when you are thin, you will eat the candy bars or high-fat foods you are passing up now; when you are fit, you can sit on a beach and never move during your entire vacation). When you reach your goal you keep the bargain you made with yourself and you indulge in all the "pleasures" you had forgone. Soon you are slipping back toward the physical condition you were in when you began your self-improvement program. Since the pleasures you are giving up are really unhappiness you long ago confused with happiness, try to avoid making these bargains with yourself as you are moving toward your goal.
- *Failure to focus.* When you reach your goal, you stop keeping score. You cease to count calories, to watch your exercise frequency or cholesterol level, or to pay attention to risks you might be running. You assume that you have won the battle and the enemy is defeated. Once the addiction to unhappiness is unopposed, it can reassert itself and erode many of the changes you have made.
- *Leaving yourself vulnerable to ambush.* Perhaps under normal circumstances you find that you are able to maintain your gains fairly easily and it doesn't occur to you that unusually stressful moments may open the door to the addiction to unhappiness. Then you experience a major success, failure, or loss and suddenly you are smoking, taking risks, eating unhealthily, or remaining sedentary. It feels as though the cause of your undoing were a sudden, startling event, when, in fact, all along, the addiction to unhappiness had been lying in wait for a

moment when you were off balance. You can see that this is so by imagining that you had no addiction to unhappiness. No matter how surprising, satisfying, or upsetting an event was, you would not be tempted to respond to it by harming yourself.

### Bonnie

*Bonnie was an account executive for a large advertising firm. When she turned 40 she realized that she was "feeling her age." She huffed a bit if she had to climb stairs, she began to avoid short-sleeve shirts because she was embarrassed about her flabby arms, and after a recreational bike ride, she would wake up stiff the next morning. She concluded that the time had come to join a health club and work at getting back in shape. Over the next few months she made exercising, strength training, and stretching a priority and was thrilled with the results. She developed good endurance and muscle tone, and she rarely felt stiff.*

*Then her boss assigned her an enormous account, which reflected her agency's confidence in her abilities. However, even though the new account was very time-consuming, she was expected to continue servicing her old accounts. Moreover, the new clients preferred to meet with her in the early morning, which was the time she had blocked out for the gym.*

*Reluctantly and gradually, Bonnie stopped going to the gym and began to lose the gains she had made. Karen, a friend of Bonnie's who had worked with us, suggested that perhaps the problem was not just that work had become more demanding. Karen told her about the addiction to unhappiness and explained how it could operate in disguise. While Bonnie's new responsibilities at work were demanding, Karen pointed out that there was no compelling reason why Bonnie had to give up going to the gym. It was the addiction to unhappiness that convinced her she had to stop the fitness program that was making her feel so much better.*

*Once Bonnie understood that abandoning the gym had been a reaction to the pleasure of becoming fit, she rescheduled her gym times to her lunch hour and on weekends. When her lunch hour was taken up with a meeting, she went to the gym after work. Soon she was feeling better, and she resolved not to let the addiction to unhappiness ambush her again.*

In concluding this chapter we emphasize that the key to attaining physical well-being is to keep moving forward no matter how slowly and to view setbacks as signs of progress and as learning experiences. In other words, as long there is breath in your body, do not let the addiction to unhappiness convince you that you cannot reach and maintain a healthy weight and fitness level and become more careful and caring toward yourself.

# Chapter 6

# Building Relationships Based on Closeness, Not Conflict

Early childhood experiences can interfere with adults' abilities to form and maintain close, meaningful relationships, as discussed in detail in Chapter 2. Children who are left to cry as babies, have too much expected of them, or are disciplined may confuse unhappiness with happiness. As adults these children may involve themselves with friends and partners who are indifferent to their suffering or who respond harshly when they make mistakes. Or they, themselves, may struggle to be compassionate with friends and partners. When parents and other important adults disapprove of children's wishes for closeness and affection, treat siblings unequally, or misunderstand children's behavior in the romantic phase, children may unknowingly mislabel the unhappiness they feel as good feelings. They may strive to re-create this false happiness (unhappiness in disguise) in subsequent relationships, for example, by picking fights or by feeling habitually jealous and competitive with friends and partners.

Relationships are especially vulnerable to disruption by the addiction to unhappiness because they have the potential to be the most powerful source of pleasure in life. The ongoing though unrecognized need to use relationships with friends, partners, and family as a source of unhappiness as well as of happiness is the cause of much of the disappointment so many people feel about their lives.

The influence of the addiction to unhappiness on relationships can be difficult to identify because it is so easy to look no further than the other person's behavior to explain the pain that is being felt. Even when the other person is struggling with his or her own addiction to unhappiness, you still hold the keys to your own happiness. People convince themselves that the other person is the problem when in fact their addiction to unhappiness has led them to choose people who are certain to make their lives miserable, to feel negatively about or provoke conflict with those with whom they could otherwise be happy, or to believe the other person is causing an unhappiness that really arises within themselves.

If you are in a relationship that makes you unhappy a significant amount of the time, it is more effective and empowering to assume that your addiction to unhappiness is the cause. You may be trying to have a relationship with the wrong person. You may be unknowingly sabotaging the potential for a consistently positive relationship with the right person. Or without realizing it, you may be holding the relationship responsible for painful emotions, like depression or anxiety, which are entirely unrelated to the other person.

Though focusing on the other's shortcomings can seem active and purposeful, it robs you of all control. You can change yourself, but you cannot force someone else to change. What you can do, once you identify the problems the addiction to unhappiness is causing you in relationships, is to try to get the other person to work with you to improve the quality of the relationship. This is different, however, from spending your life waiting for the other person to make you happy and feeling cheated because things are not getting better.

In this chapter, we include a *relationship questionnaire* to help you uncover the ways in which the addiction to unhappiness may be undermining your desire for close, meaningful, pleasurable relationships. Because the addiction to unhappiness can interfere with your ability to make an accurate evaluation of your relationships, we offer guidelines to help you decide whether your conclusions are correct. For example, a relationship that is mostly positive may seem predominantly negative because the addiction to unhappiness is causing you to provoke the other person's negative behavior, to overlook the other person's positive behavior, or to blow the other person's negative behavior out of proportion.

If as you review the answers you give to the relationship questionnaire you conclude that the negatives in a relationship are more important than the positives, the next step is to determine whether the relationship should be saved and, if so, whether it can be saved. We offer guidelines to help you decide what must change to tip the balance in a positive direction. If change seems feasible, you can share your conclusions with the other person in the form of a constructive plan, all the while being aware that the addiction to unhappiness may tempt you to sabotage your own or the other person's efforts at change. When improvement doesn't seem likely or isn't happening, we offer guidelines to help you know whether, without realizing it, you are remaining in a relationship that is bad for you mainly because the relationship soothes the addiction to the unhappiness.

If your answers to the relationship questionnaire tell you that on balance the positives in a relationship outweigh the negatives, yet the relationship is less satisfying than you wish it to be, we offer guidelines that can effectively improve any relationship. Ideally, you will involve the other person, because relationship change works best when both people are aware that they sometimes seek conflict even as they pursue closeness. If for some reason you conclude that you don't want to involve the other in the effort to improve the relationship, we will show you effective strategies you can use on your own to get more enjoyment from each and every relationship.

Many people find it helpful to begin by trying to improve one relationship at a time. Because the addiction to unhappiness can affect relationships in ways that are not readily apparent, concentrating on one relationship can make it easier to uncover the ways in which the addiction to unhappiness is undermining the wish for genuine relationship pleasure.

On the other hand, if on reflection you realize that all of your relationships seem disappointing in the same way, you may find it more helpful to look at them collectively to see if you can find the pattern that is making your relationships unsatisfying. There are people whose jealousy, competitiveness, or insecurity make every relationship problematic; other people consistently choose friends and partners who are critical, unavailable, or disloyal. It can be useful to realize that the same problems are affecting each of your relationships.

## Identifying the Positives and Negatives in a Friendship or a Romantic Relationship

The most important question about any relationship is, "On balance, is it worth it?" Like skiing, painting, and playing the piano, most social relationships are optional and recreational. Their only purpose is to provide enjoyment and make your life more pleasant. If a friendship or romantic relationship regularly causes you more pain than pleasure, there is no reason to assume it is a life sentence. The first step is to make an accurate evaluation of the positives and negatives.

The same questions can be used to assess friendships and love relationships, except that the consideration of romantic relationships also takes into account the qualities of physical affection and sexual pleasure, as well as the enjoyment of making a deep and exclusive commitment. Answering the questions in the following relationship questionnaire will help you decide whether a relationship is predominantly positive or predominantly negative. The relationship questionnaire is intended to give you a fresh perspective on each of your meaningful relationships. The importance you give to each answer is up to you.

### Relationship Questionnaire

1. *Do you usually enjoy spending time alone with the other person?* Since the purpose of social relationships is to add pleasure to your life, it seems obvious that a basic requirement is that the two of you enjoy

being together. Yet a surprising number of people don't enjoy being with the person with whom they have chosen to be involved.

2. *Do you frequently experience the other person as critical or unsupportive of you or do you usually feel admired and appreciated by the other person?* One of the great pleasures in relationships is to feel appreciated and valued. The addiction to unhappiness frequently leads people to choose relationships in which this pleasure is absent and in which the opposite is the case.

3. *Do you frequently feel that you feel negatively toward the other person or do you normally feel admiration and affection toward the other person?* Another important relationship pleasure is to feel that you have chosen to be involved with someone you esteem and care about. If you do not value the other person, the relationship is likely to be more negative than positive.

4. *Do you and the other person have good lines of communication or do disagreements smolder or immediately burst into flames?* Conflict resolution is an important part of any relationship. If differences of opinion become the occasion for resentment, sniping, or open warfare, the relationship may be seriously damaged.

5. *If the other person has habits or traits that irritate you, do these seem relatively unimportant or do you find yourself dwelling on them? Conversely, does the other person constantly focus on things you do that the other finds annoying?* In general, if the other person's habits drive you crazy or your habits make the other person angry, this is less a problem in itself than a sign of more general trouble in the relationship. When there are many negatives in a relationship, discontent often becomes focused on the "little things" that are obvious (he leaves his clothes strewn around the room, she is always late) rather than on the "big things" (he is untruthful, she is not affectionate) that are potentially more explosive to address. If the relationship is good in other ways, with some effort you and the other person will usually be able to overlook or to alter habits you each find irritating.

6. *Does the other person seem to want the same amount of involvement as you do? Is the other usually available when you want to relate? Is the other content with a reasonable amount of your time and attention?*

All too commonly people choose friends and partners who make genuine relationship pleasure difficult because they are either unavailable or overly demanding. The unavailable other constantly engages in solitary pursuits, disappears, or doesn't return phone calls. The overly demanding other can't tolerate your having other friends or interests or wanting any time to yourself.

7. *If you are upset and need to confide in someone, is the other a person you would turn to? Would the other turn to you? Do you find the other supportive and helpful?* One of the greatest pleasures in a friendship or romantic relationship is having someone with whom to share your most intimate thoughts and ideas and who also enjoys confiding in you. The addiction to unhappiness can lead you to choose friends and partners who are insensitive, self-absorbed, impatient, or critical, so that the experience of confiding in them is painful rather than pleasurable. Sometimes people choose friends and partners who are unwilling to share their feelings with them, which robs the relationship of the pleasure of intimacy.

8. *Are you caring and considerate of each other's needs?* If you were out of shape, would a friend or partner who was more athletic become impatient if you needed frequent rest stops while hiking? Would your friend or partner become irritable if you had to spend some of the time you would otherwise have together caring for an aging parent?

9. *Are you happy for each other's successes or is there a competitiveness that makes sharing accomplishments difficult?* It is very enjoyable to share achieved goals or recognition with those close to you. By the same token, it can be very painful if friends or partners feel a loss when you succeed.

10. *Is the relationship unequal, that is, is it based on one person "rescuing" the other or always obliging the other?* As a way of satisfying the addiction to unhappiness, some people choose friends and partners who need rescuing. While a friendship or love relationship devoted mainly to saving others from themselves can feel gratifying, this is false pleasure (unhappiness masquerading as happiness). Friendships and love

relationships are truly pleasurable only when both participants give of themselves. When others are mostly unavailable or dysfunctional, it is extremely difficult to have real relationship pleasure with them.

Of course, we are not implying that if misfortune befalls a friend or partner with whom you have always had a positive relationship, that you be disloyal or turn your back. There is all the difference in the world between choosing someone as a friend or partner *because* they need to be rescued from themselves, and remaining loyal to a friend or partner who has fallen upon hard times.

There are also relationships that are unequal in that it is assumed that one person will always give in to the other's wishes. The one giving in has the painful experience that the relationship survives only because his or her needs are always subordinated. The one whose wishes rule misses out on the pleasures of mutuality and caring.

11. *Is the other person generally loyal, honest, and reliable?* It is not uncommon for the addiction to unhappiness to cause people to choose friends and partners who are dishonest, disloyal, or unreliable (e.g., they disparage them behind their backs; they don't keep commitments; a lover turns out to be secretly involved with, or even married to, someone else). All too often people turn a blind eye to, discount, or overlook these destructive traits; or they repeatedly believe the other's promises that the behavior will never recur and then are bitterly disappointed. Even worse, the addiction to unhappiness may lead people to settle for a friend or partner with these flaws by convincing themselves that they might as well hang on to the relationship because they won't be able to "do better."

12. *Is the other emotionally, physically, or sexually abusive?* If so, no positive answer to any other of these questions can compensate for this behavior. If you are not in danger, you may decide to give the other a chance to get professional help. But if he or she won't try to change, or if change doesn't happen promptly or is insufficient, plan to end the relationship. Only the addiction to unhappiness would cause you to remain in an abusive relationship.

The following questions are relevant only to romantic relationships.

1. *Is the other person romantic and affectionate, and is the physical relationship satisfying? Do you find the other attractive and vice versa?*

2. *Can you trust the other to be faithful and not to expose you to sexually transmitted diseases?*

3. *Do each of you take responsibility for your own moods?* Some people who are depressed, anxious, or irritable, blame the other for their distress. Some partners find it impossible to feel happy if the other is not there.

4. Are both of you able to make commitments to the other that are appropriate to the duration and level of intimacy of the relationship? All too often people waste the best years of their lives waiting in vain for their partner to decide to make a permanent commitment to the relationship.

## Evaluate Your Self-Assessment

Review the answers you gave to the relationship questionnaire to arrive at an overall assessment of the pleasure/pain ratio this relationship is providing you now. It is important that you make this determination as carefully as possible, because it will be the basis for all subsequent decisions about the relationship. This calculus will probably not be as simple as adding up positives and negatives. Some qualities may seem more important to you than others. This is fine so long as you consider whether the addiction to unhappiness is coloring the weight you assign to different answers. You may also want to add other important positive or negative relationship qualities to the questionnaire.

Whether on balance you rated your chosen relationship positive or negative, it is also important to consider if, without your knowledge, your assessment is being skewed by the addiction to unhappiness. Distortions can occur in both directions—positive and negative.

### Is Your Relationship Assessment Excessively Positive?

If after answering the relationship questionnaire you conclude that the relationship on which you are focusing is more positive than negative, you need to consider the possibility that the addiction to unhappiness is distorting your judgment. It may blind you to the reality that you are in a relationship that is causing you more pain than genuine enjoyment. Many people remain in a relationship that is predominantly negative because they overlook the unsatisfying parts of the relationship and they overvalue the few pleasant aspects. Answering the questions in the relationship questionnaire will help you to identify negatives and positives you may not have noticed. It is also possible that you may react by discounting the negatives and overvaluing the positives. For example, if the other person is regularly critical of you, you may downplay this negative experience by feeling that the criticisms are justified. None of us is perfect, but this is not a reason to accept constant criticism as your due.

### Sam

Sam was in a long-term relationship with Maria and was thinking seriously about asking her to marry him. He would have asked her already, but he was not certain that he could make her happy. Sam was a plastic surgeon who was in charge of a burn unit in a busy community hospital. He loved his work both because it was challenging and also because he felt happy to be giving good care to an underserved population that would not have been able to afford plastic surgery on a private basis.

Maria, however, wanted a more affluent lifestyle then they could presently afford. She frequently criticized Sam for his choice of workplace and urged him to join a private plastic surgery practice and make more money. Sam wanted to oblige her, but he shuddered when he thought of devoting his medical skills to helping affluent people try to retard the aging process. He felt bad because he was convinced he was falling short as a partner and provider for Maria, and he blamed himself for not being more flexible. At a friend's urging, he consulted us.

Sam told us that he loved Maria, valued her opinions, and was devastated that she felt so disappointed in him. He wanted her admiration, and he felt guilty that he couldn't bring himself to make the changes she required. It never occurred to Sam that Maria's criticisms were unfair or unreasonable. It was quite a while before he realized that *the unhappiness he was feeling in the relationship was acceptable to him because from childhood on, the addiction to unhappiness had caused him to take the blame whenever anyone was negative about him and to feel that others' needs and desires should take precedence over his own wishes. As he became able to step back and evaluate Maria's criticisms, Sam saw that he had chosen someone who loved him not for the person he was but for the person she hoped to shape and mold. When he saw this, he also realized that he didn't want to be that person—that it involved abandoning his own ideals, beliefs, and values, and that the price of the relationship was thus way too high. Eventually Sam ended the relationship with Maria and found someone who valued his personal and professional ideals and commitment.*

Sometimes people prevent themselves from seeing the negatives in a relationship by taking the blame for the other's bad behavior. An example is a woman we know whose partner was cheating on her. Her addiction to unhappiness persuaded her to stay with him by convincing her that his infidelity was her fault—that she was not sufficiently attractive or entertaining to hold his interest.

There are those who don't see a friend's or partner's negative qualities because they have taken on the responsibility for rescuing the other. Perhaps the other drinks too much or is habitually otherwise dysfunctional. When the other is in constant need of help, it can be difficult to ask oneself honestly whether the relationship is worth preserving. Certainly, we are not suggesting that if a person with whom you have a positive relationship suddenly encounters bad times (becomes depressed, gets ill, has financial difficulties) you should evaluate the relationship as though the good times had never existed. However, there is all the difference between remaining loyal to a true friend or partner and feeling obliged to stay in a relationship that has in fact mainly served to gratify the addiction to unhappiness.

### Clara

*Clara had dated a lot of men when she met Allen. He was handsome, charming, athletic, and romantic, and they had wonderful times* together. The problem was that he was "between jobs" when she met him and he remained that way. Although Allen said he was looking for work and although he had a bachelor's degree from a respectable university, he could never seem to find a job he thought would suit him. Clara had complete faith in Allen and shrugged off her friends' delicate suggestions that he was freeloading. Clara had a good job as a computer programmer and was happy to share her salary.

As the relationship progressed, however, Clara began to want marriage and children. What concerned her was that she had always hoped that when she had children she would be able to cut back on her hours at work or stay home entirely during her children's early years, yet with Allen out of a job, that would not be possible. Allen did not see himself as a stay-at-home dad and kept saying he would find work so Clara could stay home when they had children.

Clara began to feel increasingly unhappy every morning when she got up at the crack of dawn to go to work and Allen slept on. Her friends suggested that she give up on Allen, but Clara worried about how he would support himself. She felt responsible for him and thought it would be wrong to leave him because of his "problems." Also the moment she thought about ending the relationship she was reminded of how much fun Allen was to be with. Feeling utterly at a loss, Clara consulted us.

From earliest childhood, Clara had gotten the message that she was responsible for other people's welfare. She had a younger sister whose vision was impaired, and she could not begin her own homework until she had read her sister's assigned books aloud to her. If she left food on her plate because she didn't like it or wasn't hungry, she was lectured about all the starving children who would give anything to have the uneaten food. If a friend came to her house she was always expected to let the friend play with her toys for as long as she wished, and Clara was scolded if she demanded a turn.

Understandably, Clara had developed an addiction to unhappiness that took the form of feeling good, that is, virtuous, when she ignored her own needs and took care of someone else. Yet Clara also retained the wish for genuine pleasure with which she had been born. Hence her confusion.

As we worked with Clara, she came to see that her addiction to unhappiness had led her to choose a partner with whom she experienced the false pleasure of giving up her own needs for someone else. If she wanted the genuine pleasure of a relationship in which she would not only take care of the other but would have her own needs met as well, she would have to look elsewhere. It was very difficult for Clara to extricate herself from her relationship with Allen, and she had bouts of feeling terribly guilty, but she was finally able to end the relationship. Much to her amazement, she heard a few months later that Allen had responded to finding himself without financial support by taking a job.

Another way in which the addiction to unhappiness can induce people to conclude that a relationship is better than it really is is by causing them to overvalue the positives. Many people find that each time they begin to feel dissatisfied with a friend or partner they short-circuit their negative feelings by focusing on the other's good qualities.

### Linda

Linda and Heidi had been friends since high school. Although Linda counted Heidi as one of her very best friends, Linda would frequently hear from other friends that Heidi had made negative remarks about her appearance, her taste, or her current boyfriend. To her face, though, Heidi was always positive and accommodating. Linda could always count on her to help her run errands, plan a menu, or pick out gifts for her family. Whenever Linda felt hurt by the things Heidi said about her behind her back, she would immediately think of all the nice things Heidi had done for her lately.

Linda was shocked when a friend said that she couldn't imagine why Linda remained friends with Heidi when she was so disloyal to her. She herself had never given that kind of weight to the negative things Heidi did. She began to look at the relationship with new eyes and noticed her habit of ignoring Heidi's disloyal and hurtful behavior and focusing on the nice ways in which Heidi treated her. As soon as she began to weigh the emotional positives and negatives of the relationship more accurately, Linda realized that on balance the relationship was not a happy one for her. Slowly but determinedly, she began to pull back from the friendship.

## Is Your Relationship Assessment Too Negative?

We have been discussing ways in which your relationship assessment can be skewed toward the positive. The addiction to unhappiness can also cause people to provoke the other's unpleasant behavior, to overemphasize the other's negative behavior, or to undervalue the other's positive behavior, all of which can result in a relationship assessment that is overly negative.

## Examining Your Own Role in Relationship Difficulties

It is possible to assess a relationship too negatively by looking only at the other person's unwanted behavior and never considering whether the addiction to unhappiness is inciting you to provoke it. If the other person is behaving in ways that you don't like, such as being generally unavailable, irritable, or critical, it is important to ask whether in some way you are unknowingly stimulating that behavior as a way of robbing yourself of relationship pleasure. Common provocations that can cause the other person to behave badly are being overly critical, overly possessive, competitive, emotionally withdrawn, excessively demanding, or unreasonably jealous.

### Vivian
*Vivian, a sales rep for a toy company, was involved in a long-term relationship that was causing her much disappointment. She and George had a lot in common, were mutually attracted to each other, and enjoyed spending time together. Vivian was hoping that the relationship would evolve into marriage, but she hesitated because George frequently seemed jealous and suspicious. Whenever she traveled on business, he would call her room about nine in the evening and would*

*keep calling until she got back, by which time he was upset. He would frequently ask where she was going for lunch and with whom. Once when she was eating alone with a male coworker, he "happened" to be passing by and then wouldn't speak to her for two days. Vivian, who had always been faithful to George, felt wronged and exasperated.*

*She was ready to give up on the relationship until a friend who knew about our work suggested that perhaps without realizing it Vivian was contributing to the problem by provoking George's jealousy and possessiveness. At first Vivian scoffed at this notion, but when the friend pointed out one or two examples, she began to think seriously about the possibility. As she discussed the situation with her friend, she realized that she was sometimes ambiguous in her statements to George about her whereabouts and her companions. If she was on a business trip, she would distort her reports of the trip in the direction of making George jealous. For example, she would mention that one of the male sales reps had gone with her, but she would "forget" to add that one of the female reps had come too. Or she would repeat something amusing a male client had said during a business lunch without mentioning the contribution that a female client had made to the conversation.*

*When she thought carefully about the role she was playing in the difficulties she and George were having, Vivian realized that though she felt upset when George became jealous and possessive, secretly she also felt that his reaction meant that he loved her. She had learned enough about our work from her friend to be able to see that George's anger was actually comforting to her because it made her feel that he cared.*

*Having uncovered the role the addiction to unhappiness was playing in her relationship, Vivian set out to improve things. She tried never to be ambiguous, misleading, or suggestive in her discussions of her daily activities. She went out of her way to talk equally about female and male coworkers and clients. If she were going to be out after nine on a business trip, she called George and told him where she was and that she would be a little late getting back.*

*Vivian was thrilled to discover that George wasn't inherently a jealous person, and that he became more relaxed and much easier to live with as a result of the changes she was making. Occasionally, she slipped and provoked an outburst, but she was quick to apologize for unintentionally upsetting him. Over the next few months their relationship became increasingly peaceful and enjoyable.*

There is a more subtle type of provocation that involves pushing the other person's "hot buttons." Many otherwise easygoing and agreeable people have topics or behaviors that make them upset and angry. For example, they may become difficult and irritable if you insist they accompany you to the grocery store, or they may go ballistic if things are messy. When you get to know people, you also get to know the location of their hot buttons, and it is easy for the addiction to unhappiness to make you push them as a way of introducing conflict into a relationship that might otherwise be quite wonderful.

### Kelly

*Kelly came to see us because her marriage was on the rocks and she was ready to walk out. She felt utterly victimized because although her husband, a successful attorney, made plenty of money, he would blow up every time the credit card bills came. He would grill her about every purchase and ask her why she spent so much. Then he would complain that all he did was work while she spent everything he made. Kelly felt as though she were being interrogated by the secret police over every nickel. She said that in reality they were saving a lot of money every year and that her purchases were entirely reasonable.*

*We asked Kelly whether her husband became this agitated about other matters. She replied, "Actually, aside from this one area, he is very sweet and caring. The weird thing is that when he is the one spending the money, he can be quite generous."*

*She said that her husband came from a family that had been comfortable financially until his father lost his job. Then the family had fallen on very hard times. Her husband had had to go to work at a young age and had never been able to play the after-school sports he loved. No matter how much money he had now, he was afraid that, like his father, he would suffer reverses. As a result, he became very upset when he thought Kelly was overspending.*

*We explained that her husband's addiction to unhappiness was preventing him from enjoying the success he had attained. Unlike his father, he was secure in his job as a senior partner in his law firm, but he couldn't relax and enjoy the financial security his status in the firm made possible. On the other hand, in all other areas, Kelly's husband was quite reasonable and rational. When Kelly thought about her answers to the relationship questionnaire, she concluded that overall her marriage was a positive one. If her husband's irrational fear of spending could be overcome, she believed they could be happy together.*

*We suggested that perhaps her own addiction to unhappiness was leading Kelly to intensify her husband's sensitivities about money. She would run up large bills buying clothes or things for the house. The first her husband would know of these expenditures would be when the credit card bills arrived. In her mind, Kelly never mentioned her purchases because she was afraid of her husband's anger. In reality though, her secretiveness was making him feel that he had no control in the area in which control was most important to him.*

*When she was able to get past her anger, Kelly realized how vulnerable her husband really was to the fears engendered by his childhood trauma. She planned with us ways to buy the things she needed without unnecessarily upsetting him. Even though in principle she believed she shouldn't have to consult her husband when she spent money, she began to discuss prospective purchases with him in order to make him feel more in charge and less upset. When their TV broke and she wanted to buy one with a bigger screen, she did not buy a set on the first visit to the store, but came home with information about a number of models. Her husband spent a long time poring over the specifications and then agreed that they should purchase the one she had wanted. When the credit card statement came, he said nothing and simply paid it.*

*Over time, Kelly learned to handle spending in ways that felt more comfortable to her husband. When on occasion she made a large purchase on impulse and he became upset, rather than becoming angry at him, she saw that she had had a moment of backsliding. As Kelly got better control of her own addiction to unhappiness, her marriage improved to the point that she felt quite happy with her husband and abandoned all thoughts of leaving.*

Before you come to any final decision about the quality of a relationship, think of the behaviors you have identified as negative and in each case consider whether you have been provoking them. Perhaps the other became grouchy when you took a long phone call after he went out of his way to free up time to spend with you. If on reflection you realize that you are frequently provocative, try to change your behavior and then reevaluate the relationship. Perhaps the other person will be much easier and more enjoyable to be with if she or he is not being provoked.

### Are You Undervaluing the Other's Good Qualities or Overemphasizing the Bad Qualities?

If your answers to the relationship questionnaire were predominantly negative, consider whether the addiction to unhappiness is preventing you from appreciating the good qualities and causing you to exaggerate the bad qualities of the other person. When people make a good friend or fall in love with a delightful person, their addiction to unhappiness can often spoil the pleasure to be had in the relationship by causing them to overlook the other's strengths and overemphasize the other's weaknesses.

### Cathy

*Cathy and Susan met organizing a "bike-athon" for charity and became close friends. The relationship went smoothly for a while until Cathy became more and more irritated with Susan. Although Cathy regularly* called Susan and suggested that they spend time together, Susan took a long time to return her calls and never took the initiative in making plans together. Cathy felt that she was doing all the work in the relationship and became convinced that Susan didn't care about her as much as she cared about Susan.

Cathy began to feel quite bitter about the relationship and decided not to call Susan anymore, but to wait until she called her. She discussed this plan with a friend, who pointed out that Susan was like this with everyone. For whatever reason, she had trouble picking up the phone or sending e-mails. The friend reminded Cathy that whenever they did make plans, Susan would make dinner for the two of them before they went to the movies or the theater. If Cathy were ill, Susan was always there with groceries. Not only that, but Susan was a sympathetic listener who gave good advice.

Feeling confused, Cathy discussed the situation with us. We asked why, when Susan gave so much evidence of caring about her in other areas, Cathy felt so rejected when Susan didn't call her. We also wondered why this trait, which had always been there, suddenly seemed to loom so large. Cathy said that she, too, was perplexed. We asked if the addiction to unhappiness might be causing her to feel dissatisfied with a positive friendship by leading her to focus on her friend's imperfections rather than on her considerable strengths. This made sense to Cathy, especially because she now realized that the same pattern had been there in nearly every friendship she had ever had. The friendship would go very well and then Cathy would feel increasingly irritated and slighted by some aspect of the friend's behavior and the relationship would eventually end.

Cathy recalled that as a child she had been regularly scolded for errors and accidents but was rarely praised for good efforts. Naturally, she had learned to give too much weight to the faults of others and to count other's strengths too lightly. Her new awareness that she had an addiction to unhappiness that caused her to disrupt her friendships led Cathy to vow that she would try to preserve her friendship with Susan.

*She realized that she would probably always have to be the one stay-ing in touch and suggesting that they make plans, but that this did not mean that Susan was not a loyal and good friend. When she found her-self feeling put out because Susan didn't return a call immediately or didn't call at all, Cathy recognized the influence of her addiction to unhappiness. Rather than giving in to the feelings of being slighted, she would pick up the phone and call Susan, who was always delighted to hear from her.*

Sometimes it can be helpful to view the other person as you did when you first met him or her or try to look at the other with the eyes of someone meeting him or her for the first time. If this altered per-spective causes you to feel more positively and less negatively, rethink your answers to the questionnaire. The true meaning of the saying, "Familiarity breeds contempt" is not that deep down everyone is worthless, but that the addiction to unhappiness often robs people of the enjoyment to be had with another by devaluing the other's good qualities and overemphasizing the other's weaknesses. (Obviously, we are excluding situations in which the passage of time uncovers sig-nificant negative attributes that weren't obvious at the beginning of the relationship.)

### Marriage

Marriage, which carries legal constraints and, for many people, religious and moral constraints as well, requires a different kind of assessment than other relationships, especially if children are involved. Whether a given marriage serves to gratify an addiction to unhappiness is only one consideration among many when it comes to deciding to remain mar-ried. Consequently, we do not offer guidelines for assessing whether to stay in a marriage other than that no one should put up with a life of emotional, physical, or sexual abuse. Staying in an abusive relationship is never good for either spouse, is always destructive to children's emotional development, and serves no function other than to gratify the addiction to unhappiness.

If you are in a marriage that is making you unhappy, but that is not emotionally, physically, or sexually abusive, you can use the answers to the relationship questionnaire to assess the positives and negatives in your marriage. You can then consider the results in light of your personal beliefs about the nature of marriage. If you conclude that your marriage is more negative than positive, but you decide on religious or other grounds that you want to remain married, you can use the strategies for improving relationships that are presented later in this chapter to make your marriage as rewarding and enjoyable as possible.

### Relationships with Family Members

As with marriage, many people believe that family ties are forever, and they are willing to put up with unhappiness in family relationships that they would not accept from friends or partners. If the relationship you choose to focus on is with a parent, sibling, or other family member, and you feel it would be wrong to end the relationship, regardless of how unpleasant, turn to the section Improving a Relationship You Want to Preserve later in this chapter.

If you are having difficulty maintaining a close and positive relationship with your children, we suggest that you consult our parenting book, *Smart Love: The Compassionate Alternative to Discipline That Will Make You a Better Parent and Your Child a Better Person*. In this chapter we focus only on relationships between adults.

## How to Proceed When the Negatives Outweigh the Positives

If after you have answered the relationship questionnaire and evaluated whether your conclusions are accurate, you decide that on balance the relationship seems more negative than positive, this does not necessarily mean that you should give up on it without fighting for it. It does mean, however, that you should actively try to change the quality of the relationship and to monitor whether or not sufficient change results. Continuing indefinitely in a bad relationship is like sleeping in on a day you planned to exercise—it can feel pleasurable and comfortable, and it is the path of least resistance. Yet, because in the long run it is not good for you, you wouldn't be doing it if you weren't unknowingly trying to satisfy the addiction to unhappiness.

The following are steps you can take to try to save a preponderantly negative relationship. Specify what needs to change and, if change seems possible, discuss the items with the other person. Be open to hearing about changes the other person would like you to make. Be aware that the addiction to unhappiness may cause either one or both of you to sabotage the other's positive efforts or to have aversive reactions of your own.

If change does not seem possible or doesn't happen, then it is time to consider whether you are remaining in the relationship only to satisfy the addiction to unhappiness. The emotional significance of ending a relationship will obviously depend on the nature of the relationship you have chosen. Certainly, it is easier to walk away from a casual friendship than from a friendship of many years' duration or from a romantic relationship.

## Decide What Must Change If the Relationship Is to Be Saved

Look back at responses to the relationship questionnaire you identified as negatives, and decide which of these must change to make the relationship worthwhile. Then ask yourself whether these changes are feasible. If the other person is disloyal, deceptive, or frequently unreliable, these character traits are both very destructive to a relationship and also very difficult for the other person to alter. In this case it may be more productive to (1) recognize that you chose such a person for a friend or partner to satisfy the addiction to unhappiness by preventing yourself from experiencing genuine relationship pleasure and (2) end the relationship.

On the other hand, some problems that tip a relationship into the negative column are more easily remedied. If the lines of communication between you and the other person are so poor that disagreements smolder or burst immediately into flames, this is a problem that is usually fixable if both people are willing to work on it together.

## Sharing Your Conclusions with Your Partner

If you are not certain whether change is possible, give the other person the benefit of the doubt and clearly communicate your conclusions about what has to change in order for you to continue in the relationship. If you have discovered that the addiction to unhappiness is causing you to be provocative or otherwise contributing to the problems in the relationship, share that as well and make clear your desire to alter your own behavior.

In the process of telling the other person what needs to change, remember your goal—the improvement and preservation of the relationship. The addiction to unhappiness may try to sabotage all possibility of positive change by using this as an occasion for recrimination and revenge. Anger and resentment will trigger similar emotions in the other person and ensure that nothing good will come of the discussion.

Keep in mind that the other person is not choosing to hurt you but is likely to be unknowingly burdened with an addiction to unhappiness, which makes it difficult for the other consistently to be a good friend or partner. Present your suggestions as constructively as possible, and not as ultimatums. For example, instead of accusing the other of being withdrawn and isolated, suggest that the other's preference for being alone is causing that person to miss out on the pleasure the two of you could be having. And state that it would mean a lot to you if the other would try to engage more.

## Betty

Betty, a woman we know, had spent five years in a romantic relationship with Howard. When she turned thirty, she began to feel it was time the relationship evolved into marriage and a family. Yet Howard seemed entirely satisfied with the status quo. When she would suggest that they get married, he would look at her as though she were crazy and ask, "Why would we do that when things are great as they are?" She would feel terribly hurt and withdraw, at which point Howard would accuse her of trying to push him into marriage before he was ready. Gradually, a coolness developed between them that had never before been there. Betty decided that the time had come when either the relationship would have to move forward or she would have to leave.

She talked to a friend about how to approach Howard with her ultimatum in a way that would have the best chance of saving the relationship. Betty wanted to tell Howard, "If this relationship doesn't move toward marriage and children in the very near future, I have to leave." Her friend saw that this approach would make Howard very angry and eliminate all possibility of positive change. She suggested that Betty say something along the lines of, "You know you are the man I love and want to spend my life with and have my children with. But this halfway situation isn't satisfying anymore—I want all of you all the time and I want your children. It's the only way I can be happy with you."

When Betty approached Howard this way, he looked amazed. He asked for some time to reflect and Betty agreed. A week later, Howard took Betty to dinner and said, "I love you too and can't imagine living without you. I have always thought we would be married and have children someday, and I guess there really isn't any reason to wait."

## Learn to Support Your Partner's Efforts

When you have communicated to the other person as facilitatively as possible what must change, you need to be careful that the addiction to unhappiness does not then cause you to sabotage the other's positive efforts to preserve the relationship. If you have asked that the other person be less critical and days go by without a critical remark, you can unknowingly undermine this good effort by appearing not to notice or not to appreciate the other's effort, or by doing something to provoke a negative remark. If after some time passes the other slips and says something critical, the addiction to unhappiness can cause you to focus on the momentary lapse rather than on the progress that was being made. Just as with your own efforts, any forward motion by the other is meaningful and, if it continues, will eventually result in a much improved relationship.

Another form of sabotage is to begin to focus on other aspects of the relationship that are bothering you besides the one you have asked the other to work on. This can lead the other person to feel that no matter what effort is made it will never be good enough, and to give up or become angry.

### Ann

*Ann and Carol had become friends in an aerobics class. They enjoyed going to the theater and movies together and had lively conversations afterward about what they had seen. The problem was that Carol always seemed to "forget" her money or to hang back until Ann paid for both of their tickets. Finally, Ann put her foot down and told Carol that they really had to split expenses more evenly. To her surprise, Carol began to pay for more of her share. Things went smoothly for a few weeks. Then Ann heard from another friend that Carol had bought a new car. Ann called her and complained that she shouldn't have to hear news like that from someone else—that if they were really good friends, Carol would have told her first. At that point, Carol blew up and said that Ann obviously disliked so many things about her she couldn't imagine why she wanted to be her friend.*

*Ann, of course, didn't realize that her own addiction to unhappiness had sabotaged Carol's effort to improve the relationship. Ann had not thought to praise Carol for her efforts to change, and, in addition, she had criticized her for something trivial and unrelated. When Carol became so upset, Ann realized that she had unintentionally sounded negative and critical, and she immediately apologized. Carol accepted the apology, and the relationship got back on track.*

There are any number of ways in which it is possible to undermine the other person's efforts to respond to your wishes to improve the relationship. Most important is to be vigilant, knowing that when the addiction to unhappiness is deprived of its usual nourishment by increased relationship pleasure, it may impel you to return the relationship to its former, dissatisfying state.

## When to Let Go

Your answers to the relationship questionnaire were predominantly negative and you concluded that the addiction to unhappiness was not skewing your answers by causing you to overemphasize negatives and to underemphasize positives. You have considered whether you are provoking the other's unacceptable behavior. You do not think it is realistic to expect the other person to change, or you hoped for change but the other wasn't willing to try or expressed a willingness to try but made no real effort. You must then ask yourself why you continue the relationship.

Two reasons, both of which stem from the addiction to unhappiness, mainly explain why people remain in unsatisfying relationships:

First, *unsatisfying relationships gratify the addiction to unhappiness.* Many people who early on confused relationship pain with relationship pleasure (see Chapter 3) have no other model of relating. They expect that relationships will inevitably consist of some form of conflict, betrayal, disrespect, distance, etc., and they accept these painful relationship experiences as normal and inevitable. They cannot bring themselves to leave an unsatisfactory relationship because they do not think the relationship they are in is "so bad." Without any evidence they blame themselves for the other's unacceptable behavior. They feel unwilling to hurt the other person's feelings. They do not believe that they can do better elsewhere. They are convinced they would feel lost without the relationship.

Second, *people don't have to face their own relationship issues if the other person's problems are more serious or more apparent.* If a person's friend or partner is abusive or very withdrawn, the person is spared the necessity of confronting his or her own conflicts about creating a close, enjoyable relationship. In other words, the addiction to unhappiness can take cover behind the other's flaws.

There are innumerable ways in which people manage to talk themselves into remaining in relationships that offer little genuine satisfaction. No matter what your reasoning, if it convinces you to stay in a relationship that is not fulfilling, consider whether the addiction to unhappiness may be affecting your thinking.

### Kevin

*Kevin had been romantically involved for some years with Clara and had become very close with Clara's fourteen-year-old son Brad. Kevin was infatuated with Clara and his addiction to unhappiness prevented him from noticing that she found it difficult to focus on anyone besides herself. The relationship revolved around what Clara wanted, and Kevin's wishes were not even considered. Kevin was content with this state of affairs until his friends began refusing to go out with the two of them together because Clara monopolized the conversation and never showed the slightest interest in anyone else.*

*Kevin's friends provided the wake-up call that he needed. Slowly he began to see how one-sided the relationship was and to feel that he would be happier out of the relationship than he was in it. However, he talked himself into remaining on the grounds that Brad had become very involved with him and he didn't want to give the boy another loss on top of the divorce he had already gone through. Kevin knew that if* he ended the relationship, Clara would be vindictive and prevent him from seeing Brad again.

When Kevin consulted us, we helped him to see that the addiction to unhappiness was preventing him from seeing any solution other than remaining in a relationship that made him miserable. Once Kevin began to think outside of the box he had put himself in, he found some time alone with Brad. He told him that although Clara was a good person and mother, he no longer felt the kind of love for her that was necessary for him to stay in a romantic relationship with her. He emphasized that he would never stop caring about Brad and that he would like Brad's permission to stay in touch by phone and e-mail, and in person when possible. Kevin did separate from Clara, but he and Brad managed to preserve meaningful lines of communication in the years that followed.

This is a good example of the way in which the addiction to unhappiness can hide behind seemingly impeccable ideals. Kevin's addiction to unhappiness was using the worthy aim of remaining available to a child who had become involved with him to keep him in a relationship that was making him miserable.

## Ending a Negative Relationship

If, after going through all the steps described above, you conclude that you want to end the relationship in question, you need to be careful that the addiction to unhappiness does not lead you to do it in a way that will cause you and the other person more suffering than is necessary. Perhaps the most common way the addiction to unhappiness can cause problems terminating a relationship is to induce you to use the parting to give the other person a laundry list of everything you don't like about the relationship. This will satisfy the addiction to unhappiness by causing hard feelings at best and a major altercation at worst.

Your decision to leave the relationship is an effort to improve your life, not to make the other feel bad. In some cases, you may not even have to confront the issue. There are friendships that you can just scale back without comment. This is often a good idea if you share other friends in common. The addiction to unhappiness can make you cause a rift that will create chaos in your circle of friends and require everyone to choose sides. If you just stop making plans to see a friend alone, the major relationship problems will quietly disappear. If the friend asks why you are not more available and you feel you need to be candid, you can diplomatically mention one thing that has really bothered you without becoming angry or going into the entire list of grievances. Again, the object is to improve your life, not to hurt someone else, who in any event is no doubt captive of his or her own addiction to unhappiness.

Romantic relationships are more difficult to end. By their nature they cannot simply be scaled back, so that terminating a romantic relationship means breaking it off entirely. And because the feelings involved are so intimate, romantic relationships are usually quite intense. If the other person has difficulty with self-control or if the termination is done angrily, the other can become irate, vengeful, and in some cases violent.

### Angela

Angela, a paralegal, was married to her childhood sweetheart, John, a chiropractor with a bad temper who was also inclined to be very jealous. Without the slightest provocation on Angela's part, he often believed she was flirting with a salesman in a store, a waiter, or one of his own friends. He would threaten Angela and on one or two occasions had actually struck her.

Angela grew tired of feeling intimidated and decided she wanted a divorce. As she was leaving for work, she told John to have his things out of the house by the time she returned, that she had "had it." She also said that she hadn't loved him in some time and that she thought that the reason he was so jealous of her was that he himself was such a poor lover that he knew he couldn't compete with a real man.

Angela was at her desk in the law firm when John appeared with a gun. Fortunately, the law firm, which specialized in divorce cases, many of which were acrimonious, had installed a metal detector. John was intercepted by the security guard and arrested.

*Badly shaken, Angela moved in with a woman she knew without telling John of her whereabouts and then consulted us. We helped her to see that provoking John's wrath represented an aversive reaction to the genuine pleasure of leaving an abusive relationship. As we worked together, she saw that the experience of growing up in a family in which her parents were always yelling at each other and at their children had caused her to confuse abuse with caring and, therefore, to develop needs for abusive relationships.*

*After Angela had worked with us long enough to have good control over her aversive reactions, she wrote John a letter asking for a divorce and apologizing for the things she had said. She told him that she valued their years together and knew that he had tried his very best. She wished him the best of luck finding a new relationship. John didn't respond to her letter, but he made no more threatening moves, and the divorce went through without difficulty.*

If the relationship you have decided to end is a romantic one, review your words before you speak them to check whether the addiction to unhappiness is tempting you to make the goodbye more acrimonious and chaotic than it needs to be. Your purpose is to terminate the relationship, not to get back at the other person for everything you didn't like. Remember, the other person didn't kidnap you. You chose to enter the relationship, not realizing the influence the addiction to unhappiness had in your choice. You are leaving because you have concluded that on balance the relationship is satisfying the addiction to unhappiness more than it is producing genuine pleasure.

Another way the addiction to unhappiness can make ending a relationship more upsetting and unpleasant than necessary is to cause you to waver and change your mind a number of times. Especially in a romantic relationship, the other person will find it much easier to adjust to a clear, firm, kindly delivered decision than to ongoing indecision, which keeps raising the other's hopes and then dashing them.

You have gone through all the steps described above and told the other of your decision to end the relationship. But suddenly you find that you are only remembering the good things about the relationship and can't imagine what made you want to leave. In addition, you are feeling you can't live without the other person. The most likely explanation is that this is an aversive reaction to the genuine pleasure of turning away from the unhappiness you were experiencing in the relationship. Ask yourself what has really changed other than the absence of the ongoing unhappiness you were experiencing.

## Improving a Relationship You Want to Preserve

One of the most subtle ways the addiction to unhappiness can rob you of relationship pleasure is to keep you from ever making a clear decision about the relationship, with the result that you always have one foot out the door. There are few things more destructive to a relationship than ongoing uncertainty about whether you want to continue it.

If the answers to the relationship questionnaire make clear that overall the relationship is fundamentally more positive than negative, it is time to stop pondering whether you want to end the relationship and to commit yourself to improving it. When the other person does something that drives you crazy, rather than thinking, "That's it, I can't stand this another minute and I'm out of here," it is much more productive to think, "Since I have decided that I'm not leaving, what can I do to get the other person to change this behavior or to find a way to make it more tolerable for me?"

### Colin

*Colin and Frank were coworkers and good friends. They went fishing together nearly once a month and enjoyed playing tennis and other sports. The problem was that Frank was nearly always late. If they planned to get an early start to begin casting when the fish were likely to be biting, Frank would oversleep and arrive an hour after they had planned to leave. Colin, who was very punctual and considered being* late a character flaw, was constantly exasperated at Frank's tardiness. Frank, who was always late to everything, couldn't see what all the fuss was about and felt unfairly treated by Colin. Their time together often began on a sour note which took a long time to dissipate. The last straw came when Frank was late picking Colin up for a championship hockey game and they missed the first period. Colin was so upset he decided not to make any plans with Frank for the foreseeable future.

One day a friend who was seeing us told Colin of our work and gave him a copy of the relationship questionnaire. When he answered the questions, Colin saw that his considerable irritation with his friend had been obscuring the fact that, overall, this was a valuable relationship that he wanted to preserve. Colin also recognized that if he were to keep Frank as a friend he needed to find a way to enhance their enjoyment and reduce their conflict. Colin knew from experience that Frank wasn't going to change, so he thought of ways to accommodate each of them. If they were going to a sports event, Colin stipulated that if Frank hadn't arrived by a certain time, he would meet him at the event and save him a place. If they were going fishing, Colin planned to leave early and stop for breakfast. That way if Frank were late they could grab fast food and get there when the fish were still biting. If they made a date to play tennis, Colin made certain to have something to read while he waited for Frank to show up. Colin took responsibility for planning their outings in a way that protected him against being upset by Frank's tardiness. When Frank's lateness inconvenienced him, rather than becoming angry at Frank, he thought of ways to avoid the same frustration in the future. The friction and resentment between the two men abated, and the friendship became more enjoyable than it had ever been.

Once you have determined that the relationship is worth preserving, you need to close the door on the thought that if the going gets tough you can always walk away. Knowing that you are in the relationship for the long haul will make the conflict that is so gratifying to the addiction to unhappiness seem even less appealing and will push you to work toward solutions that are much more constructive than the false comfort you feel when you think about leaving.

Leaving a relationship that provides you predominantly with genuine pleasure rather than with destructive pleasure or pain would be a genuine loss. The "comfort" you feel when you think about walking out is really unhappiness in disguise. Ending the relationship would cause the real unhappiness of knowing you have lost an important relationship that added to your quality of life. In contrast to the false pleasure that comes from thinking about leaving a good relationship every time conflict arises, you will experience genuine pleasure from knowing that your commitment to the relationship is rock solid, even at times when things aren't going particularly well. Real pleasure comes from knowing that when conflict arises, you will dedicate all your efforts toward improving the relationship rather than leaving it.

## Making It Work, Together

You can work effectively on your own to improve a relationship, but if you can engage the other person the effort will go more smoothly and more quickly. How you present the idea of working together to improve the relationship will have a lot to do with the other's response. If the addiction to unhappiness is silently calling the shots, you may be tempted to tell the other person that you are dissatisfied with the way things are going and give the other person a list of things that must change. The other person will feel attacked and may respond with a list of complaints about you. Soon the relationship improvement project will be forgotten and you will both be involved in yet another conflict.

Here are some tips for making sure the addiction to unhappiness is not in control when you suggest to the other that the two of you work to make things better:

- Make clear that this is not a threat; that is, emphasize that you are committed to the relationship and you are not saying that something has to change or else.
- Present the idea of change in terms not of what is wrong but of what could be better. Tell the other how much you value the friendship or romantic relationship and how much more pleasure the two of you could have if you could minimize conflict.
- Make your suggestions specific and doable, and avoid negative statements about the other's character. Rather than tell your partner that the person is a spendthrift, suggest that if the two of you were able to make financial decisions together, you could both take a nice vacation, buy a new CD player, etc.
- Include yourself in the project. If you are asking your friend to return your phone calls more promptly, make clear that you know it drives the other person crazy when you are late and that you will try to be more prompt.

## If Necessary, Improve the Relationship on Your Own

If experience tells you that it will be unhelpful or counterproductive to try to get the other person to cooperate in reducing conflict (the other vows to change and nothing happens, or the other becomes hurt or defensive if there is any suggestion that the relationship is not perfect), you yourself can still do a lot to make the relationship more enjoyable if you learn to thwart the demands of your own addiction to unhappiness. You can do this by learning how to avoid stirring up conflict, recognizing that some problems are just differences of opinion, and not blaming unrelated emotional pain on the relationship.

### Avoid Stirring Up Unnecessary Conflict

One of the subtlest tricks the addiction to unhappiness can play is to take cover behind your wish to improve the relationship and to cause you to create even more conflict when you are trying your best to reduce it.

### Ruth

*Ruth, a woman we know, hated disorder and had been trying to get her partner to be neater. When she arrived for dinner one Friday and saw that his apartment hadn't been cleaned, she became terribly upset and accused him both of breaking his promise to be neater and also of having no consideration for her feelings. Her partner first became defensive ("I've been busy," and "The workmen were here") and then went on the offensive ("It's not that the apartment's so messy, it's that you are compulsively neat"). Ruth's addiction to unhappiness was satisfied, but her effort to make the relationship more pleasurable had been thwarted.*

If you can anticipate the interference of the addiction to unhappiness, you will be less likely to get diverted from your goal—to increase your closeness and mutual enjoyment. If you dislike disorder and your partner's apartment is a mess, after an affectionate greeting, either pick up some of the mess yourself or make a positive request for help ("I think we would have a more romantic evening if we took the dirty dishes off the couch"). If you don't feel up to cleaning or being diplomatic, it may be better to wait for another day to address this issue. A little mess is preferable to a big fight.

Most important is to keep in mind that the addiction to unhappiness will always tempt you to choose conflict over closeness. If your partner has been away on a business trip and didn't call as often as you would have liked, when the person returns you have a choice. You can have a warm affectionate reunion, or you can greet the person with, "I was really upset that you didn't stay in touch," which will immediately put that person on the defensive ("My cell phone was out of range," "If you had any idea what a terrible trip I had, you wouldn't be complaining,") or the offensive ("Maybe if you worked as hard as I do, you wouldn't notice if you missed a call").

When a relatively small grievance seems like a gigantic obstacle to your ability to feel happy in the relationship, this is the addiction to unhappiness at work. Put differently, if you find yourself dwelling on the negatives (not enough phone calls) rather than the positives (your partner is back home and happy to see you) the addiction to unhappiness is robbing you of the pleasure you could be having. If you shelve the complaint and bring it up diplomatically a day or two later ("I really miss you when you're gone and love hearing your voice. If you get a chance to call more, it would mean a lot to me."), you will have a better chance of getting what you want and you will not have robbed yourself of the pleasure of the reunion.

You can see that when the addiction to unhappiness causes you to become focused on behaviors that irritate you and to point them out without regard to timing and manner, you do not get the relief you are seeking, but instead experience more alienation in the relationship. Because the addiction to unhappiness is always inciting you to find ways to create conflict and distance in your relationships, each moment of irritation presents you with a choice. You can express your displeasure immediately and confrontationally, thereby creating conflict and distance with the other. Or you can maintain an uninterrupted closeness and pleasure in the relationship by choosing your words carefully and diplomatically or by deferring or ignoring the issue.

Another way in which you can improve any relationship is by refraining from pushing the other's "hot buttons." If you keep forgetting to call when you are going to be late, even though the other person becomes upset and irritated each time, the addiction to unhappiness is influencing you to cause conflict and reduce closeness. The addiction to unhappiness can make it feel irresistible to bring up sensitive topics or engage in behaviors that cause friction.

### Mary

*Mary was a model, and appearances were very important to her. She devoted a great deal of thought to her own clothes and makeup. When they went out, she wanted her husband, Tom, to look "sharp." However,* although Tom was proud to have a beautiful and well-dressed wife, he himself hated to get "dressed up." He was required to wear suits to work during the week. In his free time, he wanted to be comfortable. He preferred old khaki pants and a polo shirt and couldn't imagine why if these were clean they were not totally acceptable. He thought Mary was being utterly unreasonable to focus on his appearance when in his view "real" men never looked "stylish." Mary bought Tom leisure clothes she thought would look good on him, but he refused to wear them. Their evenings out together inevitably began in conflict and often never thawed out. The biggest blow-up occurred when Tom discovered that Mary had thrown out his favorite pair of pants. Tom stormed out of the house and spent the night in a hotel. He also called us.

We asked Tom to consider whether on balance he loved his wife and wanted to stay with her. Tom realized that he really was happy with Mary but that their time together was being poisoned by this ongoing conflict. We suggested that the addiction to unhappiness was causing him to interfere with the closeness he and his wife could have by preventing him from recognizing how strongly Mary felt about his appearance.

As we worked with him, Tom himself concluded that having a husband who looked "nice" clearly mattered more to Mary than wearing his old clothes did to him. In fact, once he thought about the issue rationally, he realized that the enjoyment of getting along with his wife was much more important to him than the pleasure he got from wearing clothes of his choice.

Tom told Mary that not only could she buy him clothes, but that when they went out she could choose what she wanted him to wear. Mary was delighted. Because Tom was being so accommodating, she tried to pick clothes that were not too "far out." Tom never particularly liked wearing the clothes that Mary chose, but he didn't think they were terrible. He was pleased when she complimented him on being handsome, and even more important, was thrilled by the consistently happy times they began having together.

Each time you feel a grievance so keenly that you feel you will explode if you don't mention it, or you feel driven to do something you know irritates the other person, ask yourself the following:

- Am I bringing up this topic or taking this action because things have been going really well between us and my addiction to unhappiness is hungry for conflict?
- Is it really so important to bring up this flaw or to do the thing the other person hates that I am willing to pay the price of the loss of closeness that will inevitably result when the other person becomes angry?
- If I do feel I have to voice a complaint, am I doing it at a time and in a way that will reduce the chance of conflict and increase the likelihood that I will get a positive result?
- Is there a way to solve or minimize the problem without butting heads about it? There are many ways around the typical sore points in a relationship other than direct confrontation.

### Differences of Opinion Don't Have to Cause Blow-Ups

Another way in which you can improve any relationship is not to allow the addiction to unhappiness to cause you to overreact to the inevitable times when you and the other person have differences of opinions. If you and a friend have planned to see a movie and you each have very different ideas of what you would like to see, the addiction to unhappiness can make this legitimate difference of opinion seem personal. ("If the other cared about me, she would go to the movie I want to see," "He knows I hate science fiction movies.") All too frequently, the model of relationships learned in childhood makes differences of opinions into occasions for conflict and hurt feelings. This is one reason it is harmful to discipline children—they learn that relationship differences are occasions for angry, punitive, disapproving responses. Children who are disciplined do not learn that it is possible to preserve closeness with others who are not doing what they want.

It is the addiction to unhappiness that makes differences of opinion into tests of whether the other cares about you. Because there are two people involved, every relationship will inevitably contain different preferences and different choices. If you hate golf and the other loves it, this does not mean that when the other wants to golf he doesn't care about you. The amount of time the other will spend golfing may be an issue to be negotiated, but your partner's enjoyment of golf is not a statement about the relationship. If you can keep the addiction to unhappiness from personalizing these legitimate differences of opinion, much day-to-day conflict can be eliminated.

### Blaming the Relationship for Unrelated Emotional Pain

Another way in which the addiction to unhappiness can cause you to miss out on the enjoyment you could be having in your friendships or romantic life is by inducing you to hold the relationship responsible for unhappiness that really arises from within and that exists regardless of the relationship. All too frequently, people make the unrecognized assumption that a friendship or, more often, a romantic relationship should make them perfectly happy and cure painful feelings such as depression, anxiety, boredom, and so on.

Sometimes the joy of falling in love can push painful emotions into the background. When painful feelings reemerge, people frequently blame the relationship for not making them happy. In reality, of course, by itself no romantic relationship can permanently cure someone of the addiction to painful emotions. People unknowingly seek to re-create painful emotions because early in childhood they confused these emotions with happiness.

Holding a relationship responsible for always making you happy will destroy it. The test of a relationship is whether the answers to the relationship questionnaire suggest that on balance the relationship provides genuine pleasure rather than destructive pleasure or pain, not whether you always feel happy when you are in a relationship. If your partner treats you with respect, love, caring, and admiration, and you both enjoy each other's company and find each other attractive and sexually satisfying, yet you are still frequently depressed, anxious, or fearful, the problem is not the relationship (see Chapter 4).

Of course the reverse may be true: your partner may hold you responsible for making him or her happy. The addiction to unhappiness can lead you to accept this false premise, with the result that you take on the impossible task of being responsible for keeping happy someone who without realizing it needs periodically to make himself unhappy and may therefore may be addicted to unhappiness.

### Maggie

*Steve and Maggie had been introduced by mutual friends and had fallen in love. For three months they were extremely happy. Then Steve began to be less affectionate and more withdrawn. When Maggie asked what the matter was, Steve would always point to something she had done to explain why he was feeling isolated and out of sorts: she had ruined one of his favorite shirts in the wash, she had cooked food she "knew" he didn't like, or she had left a half-filled coffee cup in his car.*

*Maggie would feel guilty that she hadn't been more careful or thoughtful and would resolve to do better. But no matter how hard Maggie tried to please him, Steve continued to point to her behavior as the reason he wasn't more loving and affectionate.*

*Feeling miserable, Maggie consulted us. We understood immediately that Steve was depressed. We thought it was also possible that he was having an aversive reaction to the pleasure of the closeness he had been feeling with Maggie. In any event, we explained to Maggie that she was not causing Steve to feel "out of sorts."*

*When Maggie understood that she was not helping Steve by accepting responsibility for his painful emotions, she began to respond differently. A few days later, Steve blamed his bad mood on the fact that she had forgotten to buy the bagel he liked to eat for breakfast. Maggie said she was sorry she had forgotten the bagel, but that her omission alone couldn't possibly cause him to feel so upset. After a few similar episodes, Maggie tactfully suggested that Steve might find it helpful to talk to a professional who could help him with his unhappy feelings.*

*When Steve went for professional help, he discovered that for most of his life he had struggled with a mild depression. He had never recognized the depression because he always blamed his painful feelings on someone or something else. He worked hard in his treatment at addressing the depression directly, and over the next months he began to feel better. Most important, he no longer held Maggie accountable for the times when he felt "down."*

A variation on the type of relationship in which one person is held responsible for making the other happy is a relationship in which one or both partners can only maintain their emotional equilibrium if the other partner is present. If the other is absent, the person who is left becomes dysfunctional or feels depressed or out of sorts. That person may then hold the other responsible for the unpleasant time she is having and become angry. In reality, the suffering is attributable to unrecognized needs to experience painful emotions and not to the other's absence.

## When Both of You Need Conflict as Well as Closeness

Whether you have been able to engage the other person's cooperation in the effort to get more enjoyment from the relationship, or whether you are working alone to make things better, it is essential to identify and then to anticipate patterns of conflict and negativity.

It is possible that if you have an addiction to unhappiness, you have chosen a friend or partner who has one as well. This is neither a cause to feel badly nor a reason to abandon the relationship. As we said in Section I, the addiction to unhappiness is neither a moral fault nor a weakness of will; rather it is the confusion of unhappiness with happiness that occurs to people without their knowledge when they are very young. The other person is not willfully making your life miserable, but, like you, at least some of the time is unknowingly seeking unhappiness, which has been confused with happiness.

What matters now is *not* whether you and your friend or partner have an addiction to unhappiness, but what you choose to do about it. By recognizing the addiction to unhappiness, anticipating its effects, and doing your best to minimize them, you will be taking charge of your life in a way never before possible.

### Notice Patterns of Conflict
Essential to minimizing conflict and negativity in your relationships is to track the type, duration, and intensity of conflicts and negative feelings. This will allow you to identify patterns of conflict and situations in which it is most likely to occur.

The worst conflicts and the most negative feelings about the other person often follow directly on times of real closeness and affection because genuine relationship pleasure deprives the addiction to unhappiness of its accustomed nourishment. Often the bitterest fights in a marriage occur in the first year after the wedding, even though the two people had known each other intimately and had gotten along beautifully prior to marriage. Their addiction to unhappiness can cause both spouses to react aversively to the pleasure of the commitment they have made to one another.

Often happy and intimate times, such as joint vacations, the birth of children, buying a new house together, or, in the case of friends, heart-to-heart talks in which much is shared, stimulate a reactive need for conflict and negativity.

Another common pattern is that you or the other will generate relationship conflict, either as an aversive reaction to pleasure that has occurred in some other part of your life or, paradoxically, as a form of comfort when things have gone badly in some other part of your life (see Section I, Chapter 3). If a friend suddenly forgets a date she has made with you, or your partner criticizes you because he didn't like the dinner it was your turn to make, these slights and negative comments may be in reaction to events that have nothing to do with you.

## Disarming Your Instincts to Create Relationship Conflict

As you become more aware of the patterns of conflict and negativity in your relationships, you will be increasingly able to make your relationships go as you wish. If you know your partner is likely to try to start a fight with you whenever that person has had a success at work, you can anticipate the provocation and resolve not to fall for it. If you know that after a particularly tender night of lovemaking you are likely to wake up the next day feeling that you are not attracted to your partner and can't imagine what you ever saw in that person, you can prepare for this reaction and discount it. If you found your partner attractive and charming the night before, chances are that not much really happened overnight to change those feelings other than the workings of the addiction to unhappiness, which is feeling deprived of nourishment.

## Anticipate That Experiencing Closeness May Lead to a Fight

In the presence of an addiction to unhappiness, the going often gets tougher as things get better. If you and the other develop the ability to go for long periods enjoying each other's company and getting great pleasure from the relationship, your unrecognized needs for relationship unhappiness will try to take advantage of any opening. Then when critical remarks are made, skirmishes break out, or feelings are slighted, the addiction to unhappiness may try to convince you that everything is as bad as it was before. This is one of the most destructive tricks the addiction to unhappiness can play; if you listen, you may become convinced that nothing has changed and the newfound enjoyment you have worked so hard for will crumble.

On the other hand, if you know to anticipate these moments of backsliding, you will be neither surprised nor discouraged. Rather, you will see them for what they are—signs of the very real progress that you have made. You will be in a position to use these arguments as occasions to recommit rather than as reasons to back away.

Sometimes the addiction to unhappiness can cause you to undermine your newfound pleasure in important relationships by creating difficulties for yourself in other areas of your life.

### Molly

*Molly had worked with us diligently and successfully to improve her relationship with her boyfriend. To celebrate their newfound closeness and ability to spend enjoyable time together, they planned a two-week vacation camping in the mountains. Molly was worried that she would have an aversive reaction to the pleasure of the vacation and provoke a fight with her boyfriend. She made sure to watch what she said to him and to avoid doing anything to start an argument right before they were to leave. What she didn't anticipate was that her addiction to unhappiness would cause her to sabotage the vacation in an area that was unrelated to the relationship. She didn't complete a report she was working on and had to stay home and finish it. She rescheduled the vacation and this time was vigilant in all areas of her life in the days before she and her boyfriend were to depart.*

When things have been going well and you hear yourself or the other person say something provocative and an argument occurs, or you find that, without realizing it, a decision you made in another part of your life is negatively affecting your relationship, keep in mind that setbacks are a part of the healing process and not a reason for pessimism or self-castigation. With this outlook, you can learn from moments of backsliding so that you don't fall into the same trap twice.

## Keeping an Improved Relationship on Track

Even when your relationships have become truly peaceful and satisfying, you need to remain watchful, thinking of yourself and the other person as recovering addicts to unhappiness. The temptation to fall back on negativity and conflict in order to avoid the genuine pleasure of closeness and to satisfy the addiction to unhappiness will always be there. If you remain alert, you will usually be able to blunt this impulse. You will be able to resist the temptation to become upset when you see it in the other person, because by now you know in your heart that it leads you where you don't want to go. And you know that your life is much more enjoyable when your relationships are characterized by genuine intimacy, mutual support, admiration, and caring.

Whenever you begin to think that you have permanently vanquished the addiction to unhappiness, you give it the power to regain control when you least expect it—either when things are going really well or when there is stress or a crisis in some other aspect of your life. If you find yourself saying provocative words that cause a fight or feeling negatively about the other for reasons you know are trivial or for no reason at all, or if the other person temporarily reverts to all the behaviors that previously drove you crazy, do not become discouraged. While the addiction to unhappiness will tempt you to conclude that the progress you thought you had both made was illusionary and that the relationship is not worth the effort, you need to remind yourself of the gains you have worked so hard to establish. The backsliding that occurs after you have reached your goal can be a reminder that you cannot let down your guard and an indication of the existence of vulnerable areas that need strengthening.

## Making New Friends and Finding Romance

We have been discussing how to evaluate and repair existing relationships. However, when people unknowingly learn in childhood to feel negatively about closeness, they can have great difficulty establishing friendships and romantic relationships at all (see Chapter 2). While consciously these individuals want nothing more than to have friends or fall in love, their actions convey that they prefer to be alone. They may turn down invitations to parties or, if they go, isolate themselves, answer in monosyllables, look grim, or otherwise make themselves seem unapproachable. Deep down, they may be hoping and praying that someone will see how much they want to be approached, and they feel hurt, disappointed, and rejected when no one picks up on the wish. This painful experience leads them to become more pessimistic about relationships and to become even more isolated.

There are other ways in which the addiction to unhappiness can prevent people from making friends and finding romance. They may structure their lives so that there is no possibility of a social life. They overwork or they take on so many obligations after work that they only have time for eating and sleeping.

Often people who are trying to find friendship or romance look in the wrong places and then become convinced that "there's no one out there for me." Noisy, crowded bars are unlikely to be good places to make friends or to find love. A weekend hike or a foreign language class, where you get to know the other people well, is much more likely to lead to friendships and romantic relationships.

### Robert

*Robert was a successful engineer in his early thirties who prided himself on being self-sufficient. Two years earlier he had ended a long-term romantic relationship and in the intervening time had had no luck meeting anyone else. He had tried going to bars after work with no success. He went on the Internet and arranged a number of blind dates, but was disappointed by each encounter. In the last few months, he had given up altogether and thrown himself completely into his work. He had reluctantly concluded that there was no one out there for him.*

*It had crossed Robert's mind to ask his many friends to introduce him to someone they thought he would like, but the addiction to unhappiness caused him to feel shame at the thought of admitting that a nice looking, successful, professional man like himself couldn't find someone on his own. He imagined the teasing he would get and kept his wishes to himself. Finally one of his friends asked him to a party and said he should bring someone. Robert said that at the moment he wasn't dating anybody. The friend immediately thought of one or two women she felt*

*Robert would like and also put out the word among Robert's other friends. Robert was introduced to a number of congenial women and began to have a very satisfying social life. He was amazed to find that his friends were sympathetic and helpful rather than scornful.*

In general, this expression of the addiction to unhappiness is difficult to repair because it is usually so invisible to people affected by it. They are convinced that they are doing everything within their power to meet others and to form enjoyable relationships. If you have been trying hard to make friends or find romance but you have had little or no success, we suggest that you consider the possibility that the addiction to unhappiness is silently interfering in your search. Perhaps you are looking in the wrong places, are waiting for "lightning to strike," or are giving off "uninterested" vibrations when you think you are inviting overtures. One way to counteract this sabotage is to make your search much more active. If you go to a party, force yourself to walk up to a group of people and introduce yourself. Ask others to tell you about themselves. If you are asked a question, try not to answer in monosyllables. Try new channels for meeting people, and, above all, put out the word to your friends, relatives, and coworkers that you want to expand your social horizons. When you meet people through the channels you have worked hard to open, don't be too quick to decide they don't appeal to you. The addiction to unhappiness can cause you to overlook or reject people who are potentially good friends or romantic partners.

Initially the effort to become more active in your search for relationships might feel painful or even frightening. Keep in mind that the addiction to unhappiness wants you to keep the status quo. Remember also that over time any amount of forward motion will get you to your goal. You don't have to take every step at once and can feel proud of any progress.

In sum, the addiction to unhappiness can keep you from thinking clearly about your relationships, specifically, about whether to invest in them and how best to improve them. We emphasize the importance of keeping in mind that when you are working on a relationship to make it better, the addiction to unhappiness can cause you and the other person to backslide occasionally and to lose resolve. Do remember that if a relationship has been improving, lapses are opportunities for rededication rather than signs of failure.

Most important, whereas the addiction to unhappiness may try to convince you that it is normal for relationships to be filled with misery and strife, in reality the true goal of every relationship is to provide you and the other person with the genuine pleasure produced by mutual admiration, caring, affection, and loyalty. Any relationship worth keeping is a relationship that has the genuine potential to offer you this deep pleasure. Try not to let the addiction to unhappiness talk you into settling for less.

# Chapter 7

# Choosing Happiness at Work

As with every other aspect of your life, work can be a source of joy and fulfillment, or it can be used to satisfy the addiction to unhappiness. All too commonly, work is both a wellspring of genuine pleasure and also an unrecognized source of unhappiness, with the result that it is much less rewarding than it might be. If, without realizing it, you are a person whose work experience has been to some extent in the service of satisfying the addiction to unhappiness, you can use the guidelines offered in this chapter to make your work life more fulfilling and much less frustrating.

There are any number of ways the addiction to unhappiness can find expression in the workplace: people choose a career that draws on their weaknesses rather than on their strengths. If they are in the right career, they take and stay in the wrong job. They allow their work to take over their life. They find it difficult to get work done well and on time. They don't ask to be fairly compensated, or they don't collect the compensation that is due them. They take the personality problems of difficult coworkers and managers personally and feel quite miserable.

Consider whether the addiction to unhappiness is camouflaging itself in your work by convincing you that your job, your coworkers, or your boss is the problem when actually the addiction to unhappiness has caused you to choose the wrong profession or job, to undermine the effectiveness of your hard work in some way, to take on more than is reasonable, to feel constantly upset with coworkers or managers, and so on.

Certainly, there are situations in which people are forced by circumstance to take whatever job they can get and to put up with adverse working conditions. Social and economic upheavals and corporate mergers or downsizing can put people out of work. Discrimination, social or economic inequalities, or handicaps other than the addiction to unhappiness can also keep people from having a free choice of employment, enjoying their work, or advancing in the workplace. Unequal employment opportunities and oppressive employment are a blot on any society, and a just society will do its best to redress them through social policies and legislation. In this chapter, we are referring solely to situations in which people are fortunate enough to have a choice of jobs and the opportunity to advance, but they are being prevented by the addiction to unhappiness from realizing their potential to feel happy and fulfilled in their chosen careers.

## Work Questionnaire

The following *work questionnaire* is intended to help you uncover ways in which, without your realizing it, your work life is to some extent being used to gratify the addiction to unhappiness.

1. *Did you choose a line of work that draws on your strengths, or one that highlights your weaknesses? If you are in the right career, did you choose the right job?* The addiction to unhappiness can lead people to choose careers for which they aren't well suited, thereby guaranteeing that no matter how hard they work they won't reap the rewards they seek. Or they can be in the right profession but choose jobs that make them unhappy or don't offer them the chance to reach their potential in their chosen field.

2. *Is your work your life?* The addiction to unhappiness can rob people of the pleasure to be had in their personal lives by convincing them that their work must be perfect or that they must always finish all of it before they leave the office or when they get home.

3. *Do you have difficulty getting your work done well and on time?*
Many competent people do not get the satisfaction and recognition they
could have from their work because they leave projects to the last
minute, have difficulty focusing or thinking clearly, find it hard to prioritize, or don't put in the necessary effort, with the result that their
work is often late or doesn't reflect their best efforts.

4. *Do you have difficulty getting the compensation that is due you?*
Some people are uncomfortable raising the topic of compensation with
their employers, with the result that they make much less money than
they deserve. The addiction to unhappiness also can cause people who
work for themselves to have trouble charging enough or collecting what
is owed them.

5. *Even if the other people you work with are difficult, are you taking their problems personally?* It is an unfortunate fact of life that some
coworkers, managers, and clients are not people one would choose as
friends. But the addiction to unhappiness can cause people to person-
alize the personality problems of others in the workplace, with the result
that they constantly feel hurt and upset. Taking the personality quirks
of others in the workplace personally makes it hard to learn to live with
or to handle these people constructively.

## Is Your Career Right for You?

For people fortunate enough to have options, the choice of a career and
a job, like the choice of a life partner, can bring ongoing rewards and happiness, or it can engender endless frustration and misery. Without your
realizing it, the addiction to unhappiness can cause you to choose a career
that demands skills that have always been difficult for you, talents that
you don't possess, or activities that you have always disliked. As a result
you may be putting in long hours and much hard work struggling in a
career that comes easily to others. If the addiction to unhappiness had
not been affecting your decision making, you would have been free to

choose a career that better suited you, and your work would be more enjoyable and more satisfying.

Sometimes people choose appropriate careers, but take jobs that don't allow them scope for advancement or that are unnecessarily unpleasant. For example, people who could go elsewhere may spend years suffering with inept or abusive managers, poor compensation, or unsafe working conditions. They may remain in substandard or unpleasant jobs because, although they don't realize it, the frustration they feel is satisfying the addiction to unhappiness.

If you have chosen a career for which you aren't suited, without realizing it you are satisfying the addiction to unhappiness by ensuring that you can't achieve the success you want no matter how hard you try. Not infrequently, people choose careers that demand strengths they don't have.

### Ethan

*Throughout high school and college Ethan spent four to six hours every day practicing the violin and aiming toward a career as a professional violinist. He was convinced that this was the only profession he would enjoy. The problem was that his ability to distinguish pitches was not very good, which made it hard for him consistently to play in tune. As a result, he got little recognition and reward for the tremendous effort he put into practicing. He accepted this predicament because his addiction to unhappiness caused him to feel accepting when his efforts weren't rewarded.*

*Ethan had been the middle child in a family in which both parents had demanding careers and not much time to spend with their children. His older and younger brothers had gotten most of the attention, while his efforts had gone largely unremarked. Ethan had naturally concluded that his efforts didn't deserve the recognition that his brothers' accomplishments received and he had unknowingly learned to feel comfortable, that is, happy, when his work wasn't appreciated. He probably would have spent his life struggling to make a living at the violin if the teacher he had in college had not helped him to embrace the fact that he needed to find another career and to think of the violin as a wonderful hobby.*

*Ethan felt sad at the thought of giving up his career as a violinist, but he trusted his teacher and couldn't dispute his advice. He wanted to remain connected with music professionally and ultimately decided to pursue a doctorate in music history. He continued to play the violin for his own enjoyment, which greatly increased when his livelihood did not depend on how well he played.*

Sometimes the addiction to unhappiness causes people to choose careers that demand that they spend a lot of their time doing things they really dislike. As a result, no matter how hard they work, they will have difficulty enjoying their jobs and doing them well. There are people who work in sales even though they get frustrated and angry when customers ask what these people consider to be "stupid" questions. Others who really enjoy socializing choose careers that require much solitary work. Even though these people may have some talent for their chosen careers, they are unlikely to enjoy their day-to-day work lives.

The addiction to unhappiness can have an even subtler effect on career choice by causing people to turn away from a career for which they are well suited. Sometimes people react aversively to the possibility or attainment of success by convincing themselves that they shouldn't pursue work that comes "too easily" to them. At other times, the addiction to unhappiness can lead them to feel dislike for professions for which they have a genuine talent and to opt for work that demands abilities they don't possess.

### Jason
*From his early years, Jason always enjoyed and showed tremendous aptitude for and interest in organizing and running things. He was class president in both high school and college, and after graduation he took a job with a consulting firm. He was hugely successful at telling businesses how to change and at helping them to implement the improvements he suggested. He also enjoyed participating in his firm's pro bono activities. He planned and coordinated numerous charitable fund-raising events.*

*In spite of his success, Jason found it difficult to feel a sense of accomplishment in his work. Answers and strategies came so easily to him, they didn't seem "worth anything." Even though he was helping organizations to become successful and well-run, he couldn't feel proud of his achievements because he didn't value them. Not realizing that his dissatisfaction was caused by his aversive reaction to the pleasure of doing well at work that suited him, he quit his job and used his savings to get a degree in school social work.*

*Jason thought that he would feel more fulfilled working with young people and helping them to set their feet on the path to a better life. However, he soon found that his new career frustrated him because, although he thought he knew exactly what students should do, they frequently ignored his suggestions or felt "bossed around" by him and stopped coming to see him. In contrast to the business world, he discovered that in the field of school social work the change process was slow and uneven and could not be mandated. With increasing frequency he found himself becoming angry at his clients for slighting his advice and for making little or no progress. Eventually, Jason consulted us because he was concerned about how angry he was feeling at those he was committed to help.*

*Jason was the oldest of three boys. He was both bright and well organized, and he easily balanced schoolwork and extracurricular activities. His parents never had to worry about him the way they did about his two younger brothers, both of whom needed a lot of help with their homework. When his brothers did well in a class in which they had struggled, Jason noticed that they received a lot of praise from his parents, whereas his good grades were taken for granted. Understandably, Jason grew up convinced that successes were only worthwhile if they required much sweat and struggle. He had become addicted to the unhappiness of devaluing every endeavor at which he excelled.*

*Jason was taken aback by the realization that he had spent so much of his life unable to feel good about his considerable talents. He rethought his career choices and realized that while he did want to help people, he would be much happier if he could do it in a way that utilized his special brand of problem-solving abilities. He took a job as the head of a large and complex social service agency and soon had increased its endowment and expanded and improved its delivery of services. He still had difficulty feeling proud of his successes, but he knew now that this negativity arose from the addiction to unhappiness and he grew better and better at disregarding it. Increasingly, he felt happy to have and to be able to use his considerable talents.*

If the addiction to unhappiness is causing you to feel you are unsuited for a career that is really right for you, there will usually be little hard evidence to support your self-doubt and much objective evidence that you are well-suited to your chosen profession. A broker we know loved finance and had a very good track record. When he had a run of bad luck, rather than realizing that this occasionally happened to everyone, he concluded that he was at fault and was unsuited to his job. Fortunately, his clients made clear their confidence in him and stuck with him. He didn't want to disappoint them, and he kept on with his work. The next quarter he did much better and ceased to feel like a failure who should find another career.

It often happens that the addiction to unhappiness causes people to lose interest in their work after they have put in all the effort and long hours necessary to succeed. If you have worked long and hard to achieve a professional goal and you begin to feel bored or restless at work, yet nothing has changed other than that your career is going well, the odds are that you are experiencing an aversive reaction to the pleasure of succeeding.

## Choosing or Changing Careers

If you are in the process of trying to make a decision about what career to pursue, this is a golden opportunity to make certain that the addiction to unhappiness does not play a role in your choice. Try to choose a career that draws on your strengths and that involves activities that you enjoy and work products that you value. Be careful that the addiction to unhappiness does not lead you to dismiss a career that would really suit you because it is "too easy" and entice you to embark on a career that will be a lifelong struggle because it is a "challenge." *There is all the difference in the world between being challenged by projects because they require all of your energy and intellect and being challenged by projects because they require talents or affinities you don't possess.* The former kind of challenge is fascinating, exhilarating, and rewarding; the latter kind of challenge mostly serves to gratify the addiction to unhappiness.

If you are already embarked on a career that you have come to see isn't right for you, perhaps you are fortunate enough to have the opportunity to make a change (you have enough savings, or a second wage earner in the family, or no dependents). If so, only the addiction to unhappiness would make you think of your present occupation as a life sentence. Thoughts such as "All work is drudgery," "Everyone hates what they do," or "I can always make up for a career I hate by having fun outside of work" all originate in the addiction to unhappiness. These thoughts are designed to keep you from the pleasure you could have if you found a career that was more in keeping with your talents and affinities.

If you conclude that you would be happier in a different career, but you are in the unfortunate position of being unable for financial or other reasons to leave your present occupation, perhaps you can find a job that will make your work life more rewarding by emphasizing the aspects of your career you enjoy and minimizing the time you must spend doing things you dislike. It is also possible to plan for a future time when it would be possible to make a transition to a career that would better suit you (for example, when your school loans or your mortgage are paid, or your children are self-sufficient, or your spouse has finished school and joined the workforce).

## You Love Your Career, but What About Your Job?

It often happens that people will make a good choice of a career and then the addiction to unhappiness will undermine the pleasure available in that career by influencing them to take a job that is likely to make them miserable. The job may not offer opportunities for further learning; it may not pay well; the working conditions may be poor; there may be racial, gender, or other kinds of discrimination; there may not be enough time off; or the managers may be abusive, disorganized, or incompetent, thereby making it difficult for those under them to do the work of which they are capable.

It is much easier to change jobs than careers. If you believe you are in the right career, but your job is stifling you or otherwise making you unhappy, consider looking for a better opportunity. There are many ways in which the addiction to unhappiness can influence you to remain in a job you would be better off leaving. For example, it can convince you that there is nothing better out there, make you feel so comfortable with an unpleasant job that you feel anxious at the thought of finding something new, or cause you to feel responsible for remaining in the job in order to keep an incompetent manager afloat.

Sometimes a good job becomes a bad job when a company is bought by a larger company with different goals or management styles or when a change occurs in markets and the business becomes unprofitable. The addiction to unhappiness can convince people that they should remain in a job that is no longer enjoyable, profitable, or stable.

### Randy

*Randy was an up-and-coming commercial photographer who worked for a boutique firm that did cutting-edge work, paid well, and gave excellent benefits. Then the firm was bought by a huge advertising company. Soon the company brought in new managers who were much stodgier and more traditional and who didn't value Randy's artistic abilities. He ceased to get the raises and bonuses he had come to expect, and he watched as less creative photographers got the best assignments. Yet he was reluctant to leave his position. Although his daily work life had changed from exciting and enjoyable to dull and unpleasant, Randy told himself that other companies would be just as unimaginative, that he had a lot of friends at work, and that there was security in remaining with such a large company.*

*Randy tried to do the kind of photography he liked after hours, but he found that by the time he got home, he was so tired and disheartened he had no appetite or energy for more work. As time passed, he became grouchy and difficult to live with. Finally his wife told him that for both their sakes he had to change jobs. She offered to help him research other small and creative firms that did commercial photography. Randy told her he didn't believe that she would find a firm as good as his firm had once been, but that she was welcome to try. After much searching and determined networking, Randy's wife unearthed two promising firms within commuting distance. Randy interviewed at both of them and liked one of them immensely. Hesitantly, he made the change and almost immediately discovered to his amazement that the lack of interest he had been feeling in his work dissipated and he was once again enjoying his chosen profession.*

## Is Your Work Your Life?

The addiction to unhappiness can make it difficult to regulate the amount of time you spend working. We are not referring to jobs, such as medical residencies and many law firms, where the norm and the culture is to work a 60- or 70-hour week. We are speaking about jobs in which there is a real choice. Because work tends to be open-ended, the addiction to unhappiness may routinely convince you unnecessarily that you have not accomplished enough to be able to go home on time or leave your work at the office.

### The Problem of Perfectionism

As we discussed in Section I, if too much was expected of you as a child, you may have grown into an adult who expects way too much of yourself. Perfectionism, the unrealistic belief that you should somehow be perfect, may manifest itself in your work life by making it difficult or impossible for you to feel satisfied with a project. Students who suffer from this problem may have great difficulty finishing papers. They may accumulate so many incompletes that they become overwhelmed and drop out altogether.

If you are a perfectionist about work, you may find it very difficult to call it a day and go home to your friends or family. Or you may bring your work home in order to keep improving it, with the result that you have little or no personal life. Perfectionism is one of those manifestations of the addiction to unhappiness that is especially hard to conquer because the pain of believing you can and should be perfect can masquerade as the pleasure of virtue.

### Sandra

*All of her life Sandra had gotten straight "A" grades by leaving no stone unturned. Long after her fellow students were asleep, she would be up studying. After getting a doctorate in American history, Sandra took a job at a prestigious university. Previously, Sandra had been able to find the time to do every task at the highest level. Now, however, this was no longer possible. Sandra had to teach three courses each semester, needed to publish papers and books in the next few years in order to get tenure, and was expected to advise doctoral students and serve on academic committees. She had never had much of a personal life, but now, even though she slept only a few hours a night, she couldn't keep up: she didn't feel sufficiently prepared for her classes, she wasn't getting her publications out, and she was behind on reading her advisees' papers.*

*Sandra's experience as a child had been that nothing she did was good enough. No matter how hard she worked on a project, rather than compliment her, her parents always had suggestions for improvements. She had also been expected to do numerous household chores, baby-sit for her younger brother, and get perfect grades. Sandra accepted her parents' expectations for her as reasonable, and did her best to live up to them. While she often felt inadequate, she also felt pleased that she was thought of so highly. By putting in long hours and cutting down on her social life, she usually managed to do what was asked of her. Her job as a university professor was the first time that she couldn't get everything accomplished to the standard she demanded of herself.*

*Sandra's health gradually deteriorated. She lost weight and was constantly exhausted. One day she experienced heart palpitations. When the cardiologist she saw remarked that he couldn't find anything really wrong and that the problem seemed to be stress, Sandra decided that she had to make a change. She had learned about the addiction to unhappiness, but had never applied it to herself until now.*

*She realized that her commitment to making her work perfect, which she had always felt was one of her chief virtues, was in reality causing her great unhappiness. She rethought every aspect of her job, and as a way of counteracting her perfectionism made a daily schedule that set out in advance the amount of time she would spend on a given task. While she found it difficult and even painful to tear herself away when time was up, she usually managed to finish the crucial aspects of her work and still stick to her schedule. When she felt guilty at not "doing a better job," instead of letting that guilt drive her back to work, she wrote off this painful emotion as coming from the addiction to unhappiness.*

If you are a person who tends to be indiscriminately perfectionistic about your work, with the result that your personal time seems to evaporate, you may have to struggle valiantly against this tendency. At first you may feel uncomfortable when you try to stop short of going all out on every project. The addiction to unhappiness may cause you to feel like a slacker for "dashing off" a memo or report instead of spending hours on it. *The key question to ask yourself is whether what you have done meets the objective of the task.* If you know that you can't answer this question on your own because your standards are being driven to impossible heights by the addiction to unhappiness, you may have to turn to a trusted friend, partner, or colleague to help you know when what you have done is entirely adequate for the intended purpose.

## Feeling Indispensable

An offshoot of the problem of perfectionism is the conviction that no one else can do any part of your job as well as you can and, therefore, that you can't delegate because the result would be a significant erosion of standards. Here, also, the addiction to unhappiness can be hard to recognize because it hides behind a feeling of being virtuous. People who can't delegate may feel overburdened, but they also feel pleasure at keeping control of all aspects of their work. They view the fact that they have no life as an unfortunate by-product of the necessity to maintain excellence.

If you are a person who can't delegate and who has little or no free time as a result, the first step is to recognize that the addiction to unhappiness is behind the conviction that you must do everything yourself.

### Larry

Larry was an accountant who went into business for himself after working for a large firm. He was thorough, capable, and personable, and his business grew quickly until he found himself swamped with work. He had enough business to hire a partner, but he didn't feel comfortable not servicing all the accounts of all his clients and he was convinced that he couldn't find anyone equally competent. Consequently, for the three months before tax time he worked 18-hour days, seven days a week, and he worked nearly as hard the rest of the year.

Eventually, Larry's inability to provide himself with adequate help caught up with him. While working on a tax return late at night in a state of total exhaustion, he made a serious mistake that proved very costly to his client. This unprecedented error surprised and frightened Larry. His decision to care for his clients by being the only one doing their work had actually led him to harm a client and damage his own *reputation. Larry sought our advice because he knew that in order to avoid making another mistake he would have to take a partner, yet he couldn't bring himself to do it.*

*Larry was only able to get unstuck after he understood that the pride he had always felt when he tried to do everything himself was really unhappiness in disguise. Initially, he felt very angry at himself for needing our help and believed we, too, felt he was weak. As he experienced our nonjudgmental, positive commitment to help him improve the quality of his life, he could see that seeking our help had been a sign of health rather than of weakness. Shortly thereafter, he applied the same insight in his work life. After interviewing many people, he took in a competent partner. He found that he didn't need to work as hard, his clients remained satisfied, the work product that came from his office improved, and his business had room to grow.*

The first step in developing the ability to delegate is to realize that others may be more competent than you give them credit for. The second realization is that even if it is true that you can do every task better than anyone else can, every task does not have to be perfectly performed. Take a fresh look around and consider whether others could competently take over some tasks. If you aren't certain others can do as well as you at every job, you can prioritize your work, keep the most important parts for yourself, and delegate the rest. You may need to check some of the work done by others, but some part of what you delegate will probably not need oversight.

You can expect that the first attempts to delegate will feel very uncomfortable because you have become addicted to the false pleasure of feeling responsible for doing everything yourself. Rather than feeling pleased with yourself for sharing your workload and improving your personal life, you may find yourself feeling painfully anxious or guilty. In this case, the anxious or guilty feelings are engendered by your addiction to the disguised unhappiness caused by overworking. In other words, they are a reaction to taking steps to improve your life, and you need to try to ignore them and forge ahead with your plan to ease the pressures with which you have burdened yourself.

In addition to difficulties in finishing and delegating work, another manifestation of the problem of perfectionism is the conviction that the office will collapse in your absence. Or, if you manage to get away for a vacation, you encourage everyone at work to call you and you remain available by e-mail and cell phone for routine business calls and conferences, with the result that you can never relax. Again, this expression of the addiction to unhappiness can be difficult to fix because it feels virtuous. The false pleasure of feeling necessary and indispensable can hide the unhappiness of never being able to really enjoy your time off.

Try to resolve that the next time you go on vacation you will tell everyone that you will not be calling in and that they are only to get in touch with you in the case of an emergency. As with the first attempts at delegating, you can expect to feel quite uncomfortable and may spend much time wondering how things are going and be sorely tempted to check in. This is the addiction to unhappiness at work, and you should try to resist this pull the way a dieter must resist dessert.

## Doing Your Work Well

We combined the topics of getting work done on time and getting it done well because both of these problems reflect the way the addiction to unhappiness can prevent your work from representing your real talents and best efforts. However, there is one important difference between these topics: People who have difficulty meeting deadlines are usually acutely aware of this problem, whereas people may be entirely unaware of the way in which the addiction to unhappiness is causing them to hand in a work product that doesn't reflect their true ability. The addiction to unhappiness can cover up an inadequate job by causing feelings of boredom, dislike for a project, or the illusion that an incomplete effort is "good enough." Or the addiction to unhappiness can cause people to make mistakes that only come to light when they cause problems later.

## Meeting Deadlines

The addiction to unhappiness can keep people from getting their work in on time by causing them to procrastinate or by making it difficult for them to let go of an assignment or project. Procrastination is probably the more common difficulty. We spoke at the beginning of this section about difficulties in getting started on a self-improvement project. The same process often occurs around beginning a project or assignment at work.

Because doing work in a timely way is in your best interest—that is, is in the service of making you genuinely happy—the addiction to unhappiness can sabotage this genuine pleasure by making you feel bored, overwhelmed, distracted, or miserable whenever you think about beginning a project. As a result, you may put off the initial effort until it is too late to do a good job or to get the work done on time.

If you are a person who habitually gets your work in late, we suggest that you begin by reviewing our guidelines for getting started on any effort at self-improvement. Set a start date very close to the time you first settle on a project or get an assignment. Realize that as the time nears to begin you will lose interest, think of a million reasons to postpone beginning, or feel acutely miserable. Resolve that you will forge ahead regardless of how much resistance you encounter. If the starting time passes, do not let the addiction to unhappiness tell you that all is lost, but set a new time for starting and try again. Most important, rather than calculating how long you can wait before starting a project and still get it done, plan to counter your inclination to get your work in late by having the project finished way ahead of time. That way if the job proves more difficult than you think or other problems arise, you will have the margin to finish in good order.

The other most common way the addiction to unhappiness keeps people from getting work done on time is that it makes it difficult to complete and let go of a project or assignment. Usually there is no simple measure of whether a project or assignment is finished, which is why the determination of when a job is "good enough" is vulnerable to being influenced by hidden standards of perfection that are powered by the addiction to unhappiness.

### Ken

*Ken, a graduate student in history, found himself struggling to write his dissertation. Each time he thought he had finished his research and could prepare to write, another topic that needed looking into would occur to him. Three years passed in this manner. Although he wasn't making headway writing his dissertation, Ken could not resist the thought that he should do more research because he felt driven to be "thorough." When his university gave him a nonnegotiable deadline, Ken consulted us.*

*Once Ken realized that his wish to be thorough was hiding the addiction to the unhappiness engendered by the inability to finish and to move on with his life, he realized he had to take action. He decided that he would no longer listen to the voice that said he needed to do more research, and he forced himself to begin writing. He determined to leave it to his dissertation adviser to tell him whether more research was necessary. As he wrote, Ken kept thinking about stopping and researching different arguments he was making, but even though it felt uncomfortable, he plowed forward. He managed to finish by the deadline, and was quite surprised when his adviser told him that no further research was needed.*

Sometimes people fail to get their work in on time because they have difficulty prioritizing. As we have indicated, the addiction to unhappiness can make it very difficult to stay on track all the way to a goal that is in your interest. If you find that you are working well on a project with a definite due date and you begin to feel that you should really be working on a different project that is due much later or that you must stop and organize your file drawers, the addiction to unhappiness could be interfering with your wish to get your work done on time and in time to do a thorough job.

## The Need to Focus

As in other areas of your life, the addiction to unhappiness can undermine your efforts in the work world without your realizing it. Many people find it difficult to produce a work product that reflects their real abilities because the addiction to unhappiness makes it hard to concentrate, to think logically, to adequately think through the project, or to avoid errors.

### Problems in Thinking Clearly

There are any number of people who can think clearly and analytically about other people's work or other subjects, but who undergo a kind of mental paralysis when they themselves are responsible for producing a work product. They may find it difficult to remember important facts, to make an argument that tracks logically, or just to concentrate without feeling "fuzzy" or distracted. One of the worst aspects of this problem is that people usually feel that they cannot change it. Yet because for the vast majority of people the painful experiences of struggling to focus and to think clearly and the problems caused by producing a substandard work product are in the service of gratifying the addiction to unhappiness, they can be targeted and overcome.

### Gail

As a child, Gail was always under tremendous pressure to perform well. Even as a baby, her parents had compared notes with other parents about how many hours she slept through the night. Gail's parents wanted the best for her, but unfortunately they expressed this desire in ways that Gail experienced as pressure to achieve an impossible level of excellence and as meaning that their love was conditional. To reassure themselves about her progress, Gail's parents had frequently tested her. When she was very young, they would ask her what color an object was or how many coins they were holding. As she got older, they would ask her questions like how much change was owed them from a purchase or how soon they would reach their destination if the car were traveling 60 miles an hour and they had 37 miles left to go. Gail always felt that her parents' love for her depended on her answers, and the pressure made her feel stressed and confused. Naturally, she concluded that these painful feelings were good for her and were what she was supposed to feel. As she grew older, she turned to unfocused or muddled mental states for comfort when she was under stress. This made it particularly difficult to do well in testing situations.

By working diligently, Gail managed to do reasonably well in high school. While she suffered terribly in testing situations and never achieved scores that reflected her true abilities, to a large extent she was able to make up for poor test scores by doing well on her homework. Gail had always wanted to become a doctor, but when she took premed courses in college, she found that her test anxiety was preventing her from getting the grades she would need to get into medical school.

Gail turned for help to a counselor at the student mental health center who was trained in our approach. The counselor helped her to understand that, without realizing it, she was responding to fears that she couldn't measure up on a test by turning for comfort to the familiar states of painful anxiety and clouded thinking.

As she worked with the counselor, Gail understood what was happening to her and why, but she feared that she would still freeze in a test situation, and she concluded that she needed some time to become more in charge of her mind. She took a semester off and worked closely with a tutor who helped her with practice tests. Because the tests weren't "for real" Gail could usually find the emotional space to maintain her confidence that she knew the material well and that she could indeed answer the questions. When she froze and felt paralyzed, she waited those feelings out until her confidence returned, and then revisited the question that had made her anxious. Gradually Gail began to *enjoy the process of applying what she knew about a subject to testing situations. She went back to school, kept her tutor for support, and increasingly found that her mind remained available to her during exams.*

If your mind feels clear most of the time but freezes and prevents you from thinking well about projects at work, the first step in your quest for help is to realize that you are probably turning to painful emotional states because as a child you learned to comfort yourself in this way. In all likelihood, there is nothing wrong with your mind and no physiological reason why you can't use it effectively. Once you know that your difficulties thinking clearly are being used to satisfy the addiction to unhappiness, you can fight back. You can then make effective use of the many techniques available for analyzing and thinking through a project: partializing a report or job to make it more manageable, analyzing and planning a job with a trusted friend or colleague, showing the friend or colleague your work product at various stages and getting input, and pretending that you are advising someone else on how to proceed.

Knowing that the addiction to unhappiness will cause you to backslide will protect you from feeling that all is lost if a project suddenly seems overwhelming or your mind becomes clouded once again. In fact, if you understand that the addiction to unhappiness is reasserting itself in reaction to the progress you are making, you can see your moment of backsliding as part of the healing process.

### Sometimes Mistakes Are Caused by the Addiction to Unhappiness

The addiction to unhappiness can cause people to make mistakes that undermine their ability to feel good about their work and to be successful. The kind of mistake we are discussing can range from leaving out pages in a report you have worked hard on to failing to connect wires properly when wiring a house. In addition to being potentially harmful to you or others, mistakes can be career-ending or career-retarding. Mistakes feel particularly frustrating because they occur out-side of your awareness and sabotage the hard work and good efforts you have made.

In a healthy person who is neither physically impaired nor dealing with a trauma of some kind, mistakes caused by inattention or lack of forethought most often represent a compromise with the addiction to unhappiness. They are just like the lapses that occur during a diet or exercise program or at any time a person is working toward self-improvement. If you are working hard and conscientiously at your job, the addiction to unhappiness may feel deprived of its usual nourish-ment of pain and may cause a backlash in which you become distracted and make an error.

### Paul

*Paul was a pharmacist who loved his job. He worked in a neighbor-hood pharmacy and knew many of his customers by name. They often consulted him as to which were the best cold remedies, eye drops, etc. Paul took great pride in helping people and in doing his job well by being knowledgeable, careful, and accurate. One day one of his cus-tomers returned to the store to ask him if her prescription were cor-rect. She said the pills in her refill were a different color than her previous pills had been. Paul was horrified to find that he had given her the wrong dose. He redoubled his efforts to be careful, but a year later he made a similar mistake, this time on a first-time prescription. The patient experienced side effects and called his physician who checked the dose and found it to be too high. The patient, very upset, confronted Paul with his error. Paul was concerned for the patient and also shaken that such an important part of his work could be out of his control. Paul began to wonder if he should change fields. Thoroughly distraught, he came to us for help.*

*It soon became clear that Paul had an addiction to unhappiness that affected him in many areas of his life. He drove too fast and had had a number of serious sports injuries. He was frequently late filing his taxes, and, consequently, routinely spent a lot of his income on fines and penalties.*

*Paul realized that, while his intention was to do a superb job of taking care of his customers, at the same time he had been relying on some amount of unhappiness to maintain his inner equilibrium. Once he understood the problem, he saw that he wasn't helpless but could devise ways to thwart his need for self-sabotage. He concluded that the last mistake he had made at work happened because after a year passed without a mistake he had assumed that he could relax his vigilance. Now he knew that for the rest of his working life he would have to check and double check every prescription he filled. He accepted this extra effort as well worth the price. Once or twice he did catch mistakes in the making, which strengthened his resolve to be extra careful. As time passed, Paul once again began to feel competent and responsible in his job.*

Once you know that you are likely to make mistakes in reaction to working hard and well on a project, there are many ways to forestall this expression of the addiction to unhappiness. For example, you can have a friend or colleague check your work, or you yourself can get your work finished ahead of time so that you have time to go back and review it carefully. You can also keep track of the kinds of mistakes you are most likely to make and when you are likely to make them, so as to be on the lookout for them in the future. Most important is never to let your guard down: if this is how the addiction to unhappiness expresses itself in your life, you will always need to be vigilant.

## Feeling Comfortable with Constructive Criticism

The ability to seek and use constructive criticism is one component of doing the best work of which you are capable. However, by causing you to react to genuine help with painful feelings of defensiveness, anger, or depression, the addiction to unhappiness can keep you from using the wisdom of others to improve your work product.

Sometimes the false pleasure of feeling they shouldn't depend on anyone else prevents people from asking for assistance in the first place. Many companies and most schools have support personnel who are available to help with conceptualizing, researching, writing, and presenting a project or assignment. Under the influence of the addiction to unhappiness, people may convince themselves that they don't need outside input, that no one else can understand their project as well as they do, that it is shameful to need help, or that if they ask for advice they will be told they have to do additional work they don't want to do. Their inability to get help may undermine their ability to do the quality of work of which they are truly capable.

There are those who when they receive solicited or unsolicited advice from their professors or bosses, feel so overwhelmed with painful reactions to needing and getting assistance that they can't make full use of it.

### Helen

*Helen worked as a salesperson for a technology firm that sold complex accounting software to large businesses. While she was a certified public accountant and understood the software and the advantages it offered her clients, she had difficulty boiling her presentation down to a few salient points that could be stated in an interesting manner. She would go into so much detail about the workings of the software that she would lose the attention of the financial officer in charge of purchasing.*

*In spite of the fact that Helen was not making her quota of sales, she could not bring herself to ask her manager for help. She felt that she should be able to solve her problem on her own and convinced herself that asking for assistance would diminish her in her manager's eyes. Finally, her manager called her into his office and commented that Helen wasn't making as many sales as expected. Her manager said that he had arranged to videotape Helen making a presentation to someone else in the office. He said he was certain that he could help her sharpen her presentation skills and become more successful.*

*Instead of feeling relieved at this offer of assistance, Helen felt mortified. She suffered through the videotaping and felt criticized rather than helped when her manager suggested ways to make her presenta-tion shorter, zippier, and easier to follow. She tried to sooth her painful feelings by arguing with her manager and attempting to convince him that her sales style was the correct approach. Her manager said mildly that it was her choice, but that her sales figures had to improve.*

*After she left the meeting, Helen felt so upset that for the first time she confided her troubles to her friend and coworker, Carrie. Carrie told Helen that the manager had videotaped her a year ago and how helpful his suggestions had been. Carrie said she had been struggling unsuccessfully to streamline her presentation and was appreciative that the manager was willing to take the time to work so closely with his sales force. She said that as a result of the help she got, her success rate had doubled from 20 percent to 40 percent.*

*As a small child, Helen had been encouraged to be "independent" and to ask for help only as a last resort. She had developed an addic-tion to unhappiness in which she felt virtuous when she worked on her own and guilty when she needed assistance. Listening to Carrie, Helen realized that her friend felt pleased rather than ashamed when some-one gave her helpful feedback. Over the next few days, Helen used this new awareness to revisit the suggestions her manager had made. Ulti-mately, she concluded that his ideas were worth trying. She revised her presentation to her clients and found that her sales record improved. Most important, she began to have a new attitude toward seeking and getting input when she was having a problem.*

If on reflection you realize that you find it difficult to request or accept help from more experienced people at school or work, or from quali-fied friends or family members, it is likely that the addiction to unhap-piness is causing you to pursue the false pleasure of feeling "independent." This false pleasure is taking the place of the real enjoy-ment of getting assistance that could improve your competence, your work product, and your enjoyment of your job. Because this form of self-sabotage can feel so virtuous, it is a good idea to decide in advance that you will avail yourself of whatever resources exist in your work environment and of the expertise of knowledgeable friends or family members. Bring your projects to others at every stage, including planning, research, execution, and evaluation. Most important, when others make suggestions that wouldn't have occurred to you, be prepared to fight the reaction that tells you that you are defective in some way. If you feel pain instead of pleasure at being helped, remind yourself that this is the addiction to unhappiness at work, and that you need to try to ignore your feelings of shame in order to learn and to grow professionally. Over time, as your work life improves and you can see the clear advantage of soliciting the wisdom of others, your feelings of shame will lose credibility and power.

As with every successful effort at self-improvement, you will probably experience moments of backsliding. You may discover that you didn't go for help when you should have or that you got defensive and didn't listen carefully to the advice you got. The knowledge that setbacks are part of the healing process will allow you to go back and get the help you need.

## Getting the Compensation You Deserve

The cliché that people are more comfortable talking about sex than about money frequently applies in the work world. Many people who do excellent work find it exceedingly difficult to bill, to collect, or to ask for a raise. In general, difficulties getting fairly compensated are a form of aversive reaction to the pleasure of doing a good job. The addiction to unhappiness prevents people from collecting the reward that should follow a good effort.

### The Self-Employed

Not infrequently, people who are in business for themselves work hard and effectively but have difficulty charging enough or billing for their services. They may "forget" about invoicing or fail to make out their bills because they always put doing their work first. They may charge too little because they feel they "aren't worth it" or because they fear a negative response if they ask for "too much." In each case, of course, the addiction to unhappiness is preventing them from collecting the fruits of the work they have done.

### Kate

Kate was a psychotherapist who came to us for supervision. She wanted help thinking through the best way to help clients who were particularly troubled. She never said anything about her billing practices because she saw no problem with that aspect of her work. One day she mentioned that she would be late paying us because she had to pay her office rent and her home mortgage first. We were surprised because we knew Kate had a busy practice that should have afforded her enough money to live on comfortably. In response to our query, Kate replied that she had a lot of clients who owed her money or whom she hadn't billed in a while. She said that she rarely felt comfortable handing clients their bills or asking them for money that was outstanding.

Kate's parents had been very concerned that their children not grow up with "swelled heads." They responded negatively to their children's age-appropriate requests to be admired for a drawing, a cartwheel, or a good grade. They were always approving when Kate asked for no recognition for an accomplishment or, even, gave others credit for her work. Understandably, Kate confused the unhappiness of feeling she never deserved recognition with the false pleasure of feeling humble. Now, her addiction to this unhappiness was making a virtue out of her inability to ask her clients to pay her for her professional services to them. She was convinced that her help was less "genuine" if she asked to be compensated for it. We helped Kate to see that actually the reverse was true—that not only was she hurting herself by not asking to be paid, but she was in effect devaluing the work she was doing, which had to adversely affect her clients.

Once she realized that feeling virtuous for not billing was really unhappiness in disguise, Kate, who was dedicated to being a good therapist, changed her approach to collecting what was owed her. She wrote bills the last day of every month and made sure to hand them out on the first of the next month and to remind her clients of any past due amounts. Initially her clients were surprised, and some complained vociferously. Kate explained that she had had a problem taking care of herself and them by getting the bills out on time but that she had had help discovering and remedying the problem and that her clients would be better off with a therapist who could value her work appropriately. Deep down, Kate's clients were relieved to be charged the amounts they had agreed to pay at the beginning of their treatments. They no longer worried that there was something the matter with Kate or that there was something so terribly wrong with them because she didn't feel she should collect the fee that had been agreed to.

If you are in business for yourself and you have difficulty charging enough, billing, or collecting, one solution is to hire a full- or part-time bookkeeper. The bookkeeper will not have the same conflict about getting the billing done and this efficiency at collecting will usually pay the person's salary and still leave plenty of money for profit. In this way, you can both conquer the addiction to the unhappiness of not getting paid, and also remain free to pursue and complete other jobs.

## Working for Others

People who are not self-employed may be prevented by the addiction to unhappiness from asking for a raise or from asking for more money if a raise is too small. They may go for years working hard and being underpaid, yet feeling too uncomfortable to broach the topic with their manager. We are not speaking about people who would find it difficult to get a different job and who have reason to fear that their boss would respond punitively or terminate them if they asked for more money. Rather this discussion applies to the many people who realistically could get raises or find better employment, but who are prevented by the addiction to unhappiness from pursuing salary increases effectively.

If you are a person who does good work but who is not getting the raises that others in your company ask for and receive, you may feel more comfortable with the false happiness of not "rocking the boat" than with the real pleasure of getting the financial reward you deserve. This can be a difficult problem to overcome. You may find it helpful to bolster your argument with statistics about what others in the company with your experience are making. Even more helpful may be to find a trusted friend or coworker and do some role-playing. Practice asking for the raise and have your friend or coworker turn you down to make certain that you can handle a negative response diplomatically, but without folding unnecessarily. Most important is to realize that the addiction to unhappiness is gratified when you are underpaid and that you cannot simply choose to act based on what feels most comfortable. You need to decide what is in your real interest and to act on that decision, while at the same time you know that there will be discomfort involved because the addiction to unhappiness is losing the gratification it gets when you are adequately compensated.

### Avoid Taking the Problems of Others at Work Personally

While it often happens that people become friends with their coworkers and even their managers, there are, occasionally, coworkers and managers with whom one would never choose to spend time. Some of the dissatisfaction that people experience in their work lives often comes from the necessity to work side by side with people whom they don't particularly like or who don't particularly like them. While it would certainly be more pleasant if you enjoyed the people around you, the addiction to unhappiness can lead you to dwell on and be made unnecessarily miserable by other people's problems, to create or to be unable to defuse ongoing frictions, or to leave an otherwise appropriate job because of the personality quirks of coworkers. We are speaking here of coworkers and managers who may at times be irritating and unpleasant, but who are not abusive. Obviously, if you are working with managers or coworkers who are abusive, you should not remain silent and, if the abuse continues, you should try to get the abusive person removed, get a transfer, or find another job as soon as possible.

If you encounter a coworker who complains about what a bad day she is having and tells you all the problems she is experiencing at home and at work and subsequently you find yourself feeling upset and down whereas before you had been feeling perfectly fine, the addiction to unhappiness is blurring the distinction between her emotional state and your own.

The addiction to unhappiness can cause you to take others' sour outlooks personally. The bad feelings this personalization causes can linger and taint what might otherwise be a pleasant day at work. In reality, when coworkers or managers are grumpy or negative, their unpleasantness is often a reflection of their personality and is not directed at you.

### Gretchen

*Gretchen worked as an account executive for a large printing firm. She was very good at what she did and had always enjoyed her job until her manager retired and was replaced by Michael. Whereas the previous manager had clearly valued Gretchen and frequently complimented her on her work, Gretchen experienced Michael as looking at her suspiciously and disliking her. For the first time, Gretchen began to dread going to work. On Sunday nights she found herself growing increasingly depressed. She began to think about changing jobs. She went so far as to confide in one of her coworkers that she was leaving. The coworker laughed off Gretchen's concerns, saying, "Oh, Michael's just a jerk—you shouldn't take it so personally; he never smiles and he scowls at everyone. As they say, 'Don't let the bastard get you down.'"*

*Her coworker's words amazed Gretchen. Her mother had been an alcoholic who became angry and abusive when she drank. As a child, Gretchen had developed an exquisite sensitivity to her mother's moods. If her mother began to show signs of becoming angry, Gretchen would feel devastated, hurry to bed, and pretend to be asleep. Even this defense didn't always work, as her mother would sometimes pull back the covers and berate her.*

*It had never occurred to Gretchen that Michael's bad moods were not directed at her. Once she began to notice, she saw that he scowled and looked angry most of the time, regardless of where he was in the office. Gradually, Gretchen became able to resist the pull to take Michael's problems personally and to use them to make herself feel miserable. She could increasingly tune him out, do her own work, and enjoy her coworkers.*

Frequently there is someone in the workplace who is snappish, constantly angry or agitated, or who has an emotional hair trigger. The addiction to unhappiness can cause you to take other people's grouchiness personally, when in fact it's not about you but about them. If these difficult coworkers or managers treat everyone else the same way, there is certainly no reason to feel particularly singled out or attacked. By taking their behavior personally, you gratify your addiction to unhappiness and ruin an otherwise good day.

## Guidelines for Staying on Track at Work

As you look over the work questionnaire, decide which problem areas are causing you the most trouble. You have a choice of getting your feet wet by addressing an area that seems small and manageable, or of starting right off on the problem that seems most entrenched and important. Either way, it is important to set specific goals and make concrete plans in order to reduce the impact the addiction to unhappiness can have on your decision to change. For example, if you have concluded that your worst problem is procrastination, you might start on a project as soon as you get it. If it is a large project, divide it into pieces and make sure that you will finish a day or two ahead of schedule so that you will have a chance for review.

Next, be on the lookout for backsliding. To continue with the example above, you may find yourself chatting with coworkers instead of getting right to work on the second day of the project. Remind yourself that this lapse is a reaction to the progress of starting on the project the day you got it, and not a sign that change is hopeless.

As you begin to get on top of a problem at work, you may find that your resolve is slipping. If you have struggled with procrastination and have managed to bring a project in on time, you may begin to feel that it was too much work to do so much scheduling and you are going to be more relaxed the next time. The lack of a plan will allow the addiction to unhappiness to regain control of the process and make it more likely that the next project will be late.

Finally, after you have succeeded at improving a problem area at work, remember that you need to remain vigilant. The fact that you have gotten the last seven projects in on time does not mean that you can assume that your struggles with procrastination are over. If you do, you will likely find yourself scrambling at the last minute. You may not have to make the detailed schedule that was necessary in the past, but you will certainly have to check yourself to make certain that you are starting in a timely manner and that you are not getting distracted on your way to the goal.

## In Summary

We suggest that as you think about the effect of the addiction to unhappiness on your work life, you begin with the large questions about whether you are in the right career and the right job, and end by considering the quality of your day-to-day experience. There are many other variables beside the addiction to unhappiness that can adversely affect your work experience, including the state of the global economy, the local economy, and your particular industry; whether your company is successful and well-managed; ageism, sexism, racism, and other forms of discrimination. Use the work questionnaire to highlight the part the addiction to unhappiness may be playing in preventing you from getting the enjoyment you deserve at work. Then apply the guidelines presented in this chapter for successfully ridding your work life of any *self-caused* unhappiness. Because so much of your life is spent working, by defeating the addiction to unhappiness at work you will dramatically increase your day-to-day pleasure and fulfillment.

# Afterword: Choosing a Balanced Life

In reading these pages, you have learned why and how an addiction to unhappiness can arise, and you have become familiar with the many ways in which it can keep you from enjoying your life to the fullest. By now you are also aware that many of the puzzling, unpleasant, or self-defeating behaviors that seemed beyond your control actually represented unhappiness you were unknowingly pursuing. This knowledge is the key to learning to regulate your emotions and to finding satisfaction and pleasure in your relationships, your recreation, your physical well-being, and your work life.

You have been introduced both to the strategies and guidelines necessary to overcome the addiction to unhappiness, and also to the pitfalls that can occur in the different phases of the recovery process. For example, you have learned that because you own competing and incompatible motives for (1) real pleasure and (2) for the unhappiness you long ago confused with real pleasure, the fact that a particular choice appeals to you is no guarantee that it will make you happy. You need to ask yourself whether the choice feels attractive because it satisfies the addiction to unhappiness or the wish for genuine pleasure.

Most important, you now know that any amount of forward motion, no matter how small, can get you to your goal of living a rich and fulfilling life, and you also understand that backsliding is a sign neither of weakness, nor of the inability to succeed. Rather setbacks are a reaction to success and a part of the healing process. After taking our questionnaires and using our guidelines to expose and oppose the addiction to unhappiness, we hope you are well on your way to making your life significantly happier and more fulfilling.

We would like to focus briefly on the danger that, in the end, the addiction to unhappiness will sabotage the gains you have made by causing you to overemphasize some aspects of your life and neglect others. You may have learned to be more successful at work, but you put in so much time at your job that you have no time left for relationships or for staying fit. You may have succeeded in improving your relationships, but you continue to believe that mood swings and frequent depression are an inevitable part of life. You may have discovered the joy of being physically fit, but you spend so much time exercising that you neglect your work or your important relationships.

Once you improve the specific parts of your life that need attention, your last challenge is to step back and evaluate how well the various facets of your life fit together. Take an inventory of the different areas of your life. Is the addiction to unhappiness causing you to ignore or accept unhappiness in one or more of these areas as a trade-off for pleasure in other areas? If so, go back to the strategies and guidelines discussed in previous pages and address the parts of your life that are being neglected or that are unsatisfying. Keep in mind that one way the addiction to unhappiness has of robbing you of real pleasure is to let you succeed in one aspect of your life while simultaneously causing you to make yourself unhappy in some other area.

We close with the reminder that the inborn joy and optimism that you possessed at birth can never be extinguished by the addiction to unhappiness. It is true that if your emotional needs weren't met when you were a young child, at that point you lacked the ability to resist the confusion of unhappiness with happiness that caused you unknowingly to develop an addiction to unhappiness. But, as an adult, you are never too old and it is never too late to identify and recover from the addiction to unhappiness and embark on a life filled with satisfaction, genuine pleasure, and unshakable inner well-being.

While chance affects all of us to varying degrees, chance does not have to determine the true quality of our lives. You have the capability to conquer the addiction to unhappiness, and once you do, the most unfortunate of chance events will lack the power to undo your inner equilibrium or to cause you to seek comfort by turning on yourself or others. Over time, as you increasingly experience the true pleasure of creating a rich and fulfilling life and you become accomplished at avoiding all self-caused unhappiness, the long-standing appeal of unhappiness will pale. You will discover that with minimal vigilance you will be able to make positive, rewarding choices in every area of your life and to discover the happiness and fulfillment you were born to know.

# Glossary

**Addiction to Unhappiness**    Consciously seeking only happiness, but unknowingly requiring some degree of discomfort to maintain a sense of inner balance.

**Appropriate Unhappiness**    A realistic response to a genuinely upsetting event.

**Aversive Reaction to Pleasure**    In the presence of an addiction to unhappiness, experiences of genuine pleasure are followed by the unrecognized need to experience unhappiness.

**Backsliding**    Difficulty following through on a resolution. For the individual with an addiction to unhappiness, not only is backsliding inevitable, it is a part of the healing process.

**Discipline**    Attaching unpleasant consequences to the management of children's behavior

**False Pleasure**    Experiences that feel enjoyable or comfortable but that actually represent unhappiness that has been mistaken for happiness.

**Genuine Pleasure**    The well-founded inner certainty that you are loving and loveable, as well as the actualization of constructive, appropriate life choices. Genuine pleasure always enhances your life—it is never harmful to you or to others.

**Gratuitous Unhappiness**    An overreaction or sought-for experience that is used to satisfy the addiction to unhappiness.

**Identification**    The attempt to be just like people who are important to us.

**Loving Regulation**    Managing children's behavior without adding any additional unhappiness or depriving children of parental warmth and admiration

**Progress**    More successes than failures over time.

**Relationship Ideal**    An identification with the way your parents treated you, each other, friends, and strangers.

# Index

**Martha Heineman Pieper** received her Ph.D. from the University of Chicago and her B.A. from Radcliffe College, from which she graduated Phi Beta Kappa and Magna Cum Laude. Dr. Pieper has served on the editorial boards of Social Work and Smith College Studies in Social Work and has published extensively in academic and professional journals.

**William J. Pieper** received his B.S. and M.D. degrees from the University of Illinois. He did a residency in adult and child psychiatry at the Illinois Neuropsychiatric Institute and the Chicago Institute for Juvenile Research. In 1975 he graduated from the Chicago Institute for Psychoanalysis with a certificate in child and adult psychoanalysis. He has been on the faculty of the Chicago Institute for Psychoanalysis and has taught at the University of Chicago School of Social Service Administration.

For over twenty-five years, the Piepers have each been in private practice treating children, adolescents, and adults; counseling parents; supervising other mental health professionals, and doing clinical research. They are the authors of Smart Love: The Compassionate Alternative to Discipline That Will Make You a Better Parent and Your Child a Better Person. They live in Chicago and have a blended family of five children.